The Changing
HORNCHURCH

The Old Harrow Inn, Hornchurch Road, demolished 1894. (London Borough of Havering)

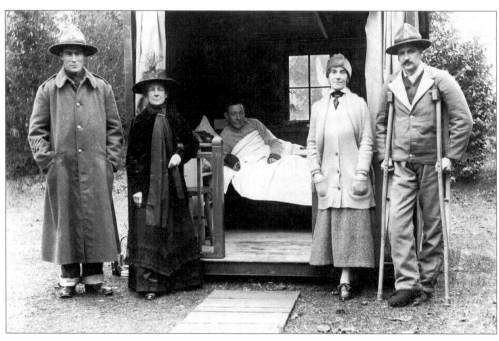

Nurses and patients from the New Zealand Forces, Grey Towers, *c.* 1918.

The Changing Face of
HORNCHURCH

TONY BENTON

SUTTON PUBLISHING

This book was first published in 1999 by
Sutton Publishing, an imprint of NPI Media Group
Cirencester Road · Stroud ·Gloucestershire · GL6 8PE

First published 1999

Reprinted in 2001, 2006, 2007

British Library Cataloguing in Publication Data
A catalogue record for this book is available from the British Library.

ISBN 978-0-7509-2039-1

Typeset in 12/15 Perpetua.
Typesetting and origination by
Sutton Publishing.
Printed and bound in England.

1. INTRODUCTION

What is Hornchurch and what does it mean to its people, now and in the past? How have the changes to the face of the village and parish in the last century or so come about, and who were the people involved? Where buildings have survived against the odds, what is their history? How did the villagers in the past live, work and play? These are just some of the questions that this modern history of Hornchurch attempts to answer as we prepare for the Millennium.

The parish of Hornchurch covered in this book itself requires some definition. The village of Hornchurch is one of a series of settlements which grew up along the well-drained gravel terrace separating the low-lying Thames-side marshes to the south from the heavy London clay to the north. Along this terrace an ancient trackway or Green Lane ran east from Ilford across Bentry or Beacontree Heath in Dagenham parish, through Rush Green, entering Hornchurch parish from the west, close to the ford over the River Rom. Continuing through Hornchurch the route is mainly known as the Hornchurch Road to the west and east of the village, the High Street in the village itself and Church Hill from the village to Wingletye Lane. Continuing eastwards this ancient

Part of the medieval Hornchurch High Street, including the old archway, in the early years of this century. (Miss H. Halestrap)

route passes through Upminster, before reaching Horndon in the east. From the thirteenth century onwards this was often called the road from Hornchurch to London, the City being about 13 miles to the west.

From the nineteenth century the parish of Hornchurch comprised some 6,783 acres. This was less than half the size of the original Hornchurch parish which had extended to some 16,100 acres and was one and the same as the ancient royal manor and liberty of Havering. The northern area of this ancient manor comprised Romford and Havering-atte-Bower, each of which later became separate parishes rather than controlled by the Hornchurch parish vestry. The remaining Hornchurch parish was some 6½ miles from north to south and 2½ miles wide from east to west. This book does not deal with the largely self-contained community of Harold Wood, the most northerly remaining part of the parish of Hornchurch.

Much of the southern part of Hornchurch is defined by its physical boundaries along the River Thames and its minor tributaries. It is not always realised that Hornchurch is actually a parish on the banks of the Thames, partly because the village itself is about 4 miles from its riverside boundary, which many people associate with neighbouring Rainham. From the Thames the marshland southern part of Hornchurch parish, known as South Hornchurch or South End, is separated from its westerly neighbour Dagenham by the boundary of the River Beam or Rom, as it is known near Romford. To the east

The parish church of St Andrew.

As late as 1846 there were tanyards at the rear of the round-topped Page Calnan building in the centre of this picture.

the River Ingrebourne forms much of the long eastern boundary, firstly with Rainham and then, further north, with Upminster. On the western border, north of the current Roneo Corner, the boundary, now with Romford, leaves the Rom and moves north-east along Hornchurch Road, now known as South Street. The border then follows a meandering and sometimes indistinct route along, or occasionally to the north of, Brentwood Road up to the Drill roundabout, from where it runs north along Balgores Lane, before striking north-east through Ardleigh Green.

Although Essex is generally regarded as flat the topography of Hornchurch is undulating and fairly high. The central part of Hornchurch is defined to the west and east by the valleys of the Rom and Ingrebourne, while the lesser valley of the Ravensbourne Brook, a feeder stream of the Rom to the west of the village, also adds to the rolling nature along the main east–west road route. The parish church of St Andrew stands on top of a hillock, some 118 feet above sea level, and from here the road descends towards the Ingrebourne.

Although there is some evidence of ancient man around Hornchurch church and of a Roman settlement at Mardyke Farm, in South Hornchurch, the origins of the main village site remain obscure. The village probably dates from Saxon times and was certainly well established by the middle of the twelfth century. At the time of the Domesday Survey in 1086 Hornchurch was enumerated as part of the extensive royal manor of Havering but by the early thirteenth century there was a flourishing community, with an important leather industry. This gave employment to a large number of fellmongers, skinners and tanners who carried out a trade in currying and leather-dressing, whose goods found an outlet through Romford's market, which was granted its charter in 1247 for the main purpose of carrying out the leather trade. Hornchurch's leather industry continued for over six centuries, during which time the High Street was known as Pell or Pelt Street. As late as 1846 tanning was still being carried out just yards from the busy Pell Street. In that year there were tanyards at the rear of buildings behind what later became Page Calnan's builders' merchants and others further east, while the fellmongers' pits of Messrs Bright and Beardwell, the last tanners in Hornchurch, were sited in a yard behind the King's Head Inn.

The old road routes in the largely rural parish have been preserved despite the twentieth-century suburban developments. From the village centre two roads – Billet Lane and North Street – ran northwards, merging at Butts Green and continuing to the hamlet of Hardley (later Ardleigh) Green and on to Harold Wood. On the west of the parish a north–south route followed the edges of the Rom or Beam valley, running south from Romford as Hornchurch Road and continuing past Haveringwell hamlet as Rainham Road, reaching the settlement at South End and the road from Dagenham to Rainham. South End hamlet was also reached by the road which started west of Hornchurch village as Abbs Cross Lane (mentioned in 1514), becoming South End Road further south, continuing on to Rainham village and then towards Tilbury. To the east of Hornchurch village Suttons (now Station) Lane ran southwards. Until the 1830s a gate across the roadway formed a barrier and the fine old house nearby, not surprisingly, was known as Suttons Gate (demolished in July 1936). South of this the road ran only to Suttons Farm. Between the thirteenth and fifteenth centuries Suttons Lane was known as Lake Street, taking its name from a lake probably sited south of the current Hornchurch Station on what was later the railway sidings.

On the east of the parish, a north–south route followed the Hornchurch side of the Ingrebourne valley. Hacton Lane crossed into Hornchurch from Upminster over Hacton Bridge, running north past Hacton hamlet to join Hornchurch Road at the Four Wantz Way or Doggett's Corner. This presumably took its name from Mr Doggett, churchwarden in 1779, who is thought to have lived at Dury Falls House. The still-surviving timber-framed Dury Falls, which stands on the junction of Hornchurch Road and Wingletye Lane, dating to the early sixteenth century, is thought to be the oldest house in the village. It probably took its name from a family named Durrifall, named in the parish registers in the sixteenth century. The Grade II listed house was threatened with demolition in 1972, to be replaced with a block of flats, but was saved by extensive protests locally. It was sold and extended, and converted into a nursing home. Wingletye Lane, originally known as Hay Street as early as 1438, runs northwards to reach Hay Green hamlet, close to the surviving Lilliputs Farm, and continues north to join the main London to Colchester road, the north-east boundary of Hornchurch parish.

The building of the London to Colchester Great Eastern Railway line in 1839 brought the new rail route through the north of the parish in Harold Wood but a

The ancient Dury Falls House on the junction of Wingletye Lane. (Miss H. Halestrap)

station was only added there in 1868 after house building had started on the former Gubbins Farm. This provided parishioners with an alternative to the station at Romford. Hornchurch Station was only added to the growing railway network in 1885 when the London, Tilbury and Southend Railway was extended eastwards to Upminster, and then on to Pitsea. A further rail link came in 1893 when a rail route between Romford and Grays opened but it was not until 1909 that Hornchurch rail travellers benefited from the addition of Emerson Park and Great Nelmes Halt. The opening of Squirrels Heath (later named Gidea Park) Station on the Great Eastern line in 1910 offered another alternative to those living in Ardleigh Green. Further improvements to the rail network had to wait until the 1930s when the electrification of the Barking to Upminster route led to another station at Upminster Bridge, just in Hornchurch parish, with the opening of Elm Park Station in 1935 as part of that estate's development.

From the seventeenth to the nineteenth centuries Hornchurch became a popular place of residence for many gentry, who built or improved houses around the village area. One such resident was Sir Francis Prujean, President of the Royal College of Surgeons, who lived at Suttons Gate (d. 1666). Prujean was a Roman Catholic, as was another former resident Job Alibone, an official in the London Post Office, who lived at Fairkytes in the late seventeenth century. In 1651 Thomas Withering of Nelmes, Postmaster General to Charles I, died on his way to St Andrew's church, where his wall monument with its long inscription can be seen.

To the local parish historian C.T. Perfect, writing in 1912, Hornchurch was a 'beauty spot in Essex, not far from London town' which he described as

> . . . a pretty little village, with a church upon a hill,
> And hard by is a lovely dell, and at the end a mill.

The 'pretty little village', 'church upon a hill' and 'lovely dell' (known as the Mill field), are covered in later chapters but perhaps a little should be said here about Hornchurch's mill. It is likely that few mill sites have an authentic pedigree dating back so far. A windmill in the mill field, mentioned as early as 1262, was probably the predecessor of Hornchurch mill leased out by New College, Oxford, along with the Rectory in 1494. In the sixteenth and early seventeenth centuries the mill was leased by the Leggatt family of Hornchurch Hall. It had apparently disappeared by about 1618 but was rebuilt shortly before 1666, continuing to operate on the same site for almost the next 250 years.

   The last millers were members of the Howard family. Thomas Howard came to Hornchurch in 1822 to work for Mr John Bearblock of Hornchurch Hall, when he took possession of the mill, and carried on there through several changes of tenant over many years. A separate steam mill was added adjacent to the windmill shortly after 1861 when Edward Mitchell became lessee. Thomas C. Howard and his brother George took over the lease in 1897 and operated the mills until 1912, by which time the sails and other parts of the structure were unsafe. The steam machinery was dismantled and disposed of a few years later. The derelict post mill was burnt down on a summer Saturday in June 1921 when a hedge fire, started by an unknown careless person, quickly got out of control and flames engulfed and destroyed the mill. Fire-fighting

Emerson Park and Great Nelmes Halt, a few years after its opening in 1909.

Hornchurch mill, *c.* 1908.

efforts were concentrated successfully on saving the adjacent Grade II listed mill cottage, of seventeenth-century origins with an eighteenth- or nineteenth-century panelled room. Hornchurch's 'lovely dell' was itself effectively destroyed in 1965 when the Central Electricity Generating Board installed a massive and unsightly electricity transformer station, despite local objections.

2. A Perfect Heritage

I have not been concerned to set out in chronological order a record of ancient local history, but my object has rather been to put together some of the most interesting facts and incidents connected with the village of Hornchurch and its inhabitants, not only in the long past, but also in the immediate past and present. It has been my endeavour to put such incidents into what I hope may be considered a concise and convenient book of reference. I have given considerable attention to the more recent events surrounding our village life, and, if it should be thought that some of the incidents narrated appear to be of a common-place order, it must be borne in mind that future generations may be greatly interested in them, as we are to-day in the happenings of a few centuries ago.

Ye Olde Village of Hornchurch
by Charles Thomas Perfect (1917)

Hornchurch High Street in the early years of this century soon after C.T. Perfect arrived.

It is more than appropriate for any history of Hornchurch to begin with a reference to the village's foremost local historian Charles Thomas Perfect, whose research and published works on Hornchurch documented so well the history up to the first two decades of this century. In particular, anyone who had an ancestor in Hornchurch at that time will almost certainly find one or more references to them in Perfect's work.

His first contribution, a quirky little volume titled *Our Village*, was published in 1912. It consisted of a series of poems and prose pieces giving 'accounts of the momentous doings of 1910, 1911 and 1912', with references to many villagers, particularly in the section on 'Our village "Who's who"' and the piece on the Coronation celebrations of 1911. This first effort was surpassed by Perfect's *Ye Olde Village of Hornchurch*, brought out in 1917 when the village was the host to the New Zealand forces at Grey Towers, many of whom had a keen interest in finding out more about the place where fate had placed them. Perfect's small (150 or so pages) but well-illustrated book manages to balance the antiquarian interest with recording the main influences on village life in the Edwardian and pre-war period. But Perfect's final major work, *Hornchurch During the Great War* (1920), must take pride of place. It records in considerable detail parish life during the period of the hostilities, preserving for posterity the war efforts and activities of hundreds of villagers.

From his writings, it is clear that C.T. Perfect had great affection for the village. It is all the more surprising that he originated from Surrey, only coming to Hornchurch in about 1902 when already in his late thirties. Charles Thomas Perfect was born on 16 February 1864 at Cobham, Surrey, the eighth of the nine surviving children of William and Elizabeth, née Chamberlain. William Perfect was then a police constable with the Surrey

Constabulary, which he had joined in 1856 after an earlier period in the Essex Police, which had included a short posting at Romford in 1850/1. He ended his career as an inspector based at Weybridge, where he remained until his retirement in 1873.

On leaving school around 1877 the young Charles seems to have embarked on a career within the cement industry, which he followed with increasing success over the next fifty-six years until his retirement. By his own account Charles Perfect met his future wife Ellen Mary Elizabeth Williams when he was 'sweet seventeen' and he 'at once set out to court her'. This places their meeting to 1881 when he was lodging at Lambeth Road, Vauxhall, employed as a clerk, while Ellen lived close by with her parents, Michael and Eleanor Williams. By 1891 Charles was living with his parents at Weybridge, described as a shorthand clerk almost certainly using the system perfected by Isaac Pitman. His ten-year courtship of 'Nellie', as she was known, finally ended on 21 September 1891 when they were married at the parish church of Kenwyn, near Truro, Cornwall. Ellen's parents had retired to Cornwall, from where they had originated.

The newly-wed Perfects set up home at Weybridge, where their daughter Dora was born the following year at Kenwyn, Portmore Park – the house no doubt named to reflect Ellen's Cornish connections. What prompted the move to Hornchurch remains unclear but it may have been linked to Charles' developing career. The Portland cement industry in which he was employed faced great upheaval in 1900 when the Associated Portland Cement Manufacturers Ltd. was formed through the merger of twenty-four independent companies. One of these was the New Rainham Portland Cement Company, whose works were on Mud Island in the Hornchurch marshes. The new company had its headquarters at 72 Fenchurch Street and this may have prompted Charles Perfect to relocate to a village with direct rail access to the nearby station.

In 1902 Charles Perfect bought a pair of newly built semi-detached houses in Station Road (now Station Lane), Hornchurch, for £270, living in one of these which the Perfects named Weylands, perhaps in reminiscence of their Weybridge links. This was only a short walk from Hornchurch Station from where C.T. Perfect went 'off every morning to town with a lot of other chaps'. The Perfect's tenants and next door neighbours were Robert Living and family.

The Perfects were soon engaged in village activities, with Charles serving as bandmaster to the Church Lads Brigade, formed in 1903 – although it is unclear whether this was an indication of his musical or organisational ability. He was also, along with other villagers, an occasional member, under the name of 'Uncle Bones', of the 'Haughty-Cultured Crows Nigger Minstrel Troupe' which is known to have performed three times up to 1912.

By 1912 Perfect was immersed enough in village life to be able to write poems, prose pieces and pen-pictures about village activities, happenings and many local individuals. These were included in his *Our Village*, which he published privately that year with the encouragement of his friends in the village. He was probably already collecting material for a parish history which he said in September 1917 he had 'been

Station Lane, Hornchurch, close to Perfect's house, Weylands.

engaged on for several years, but war prices and conditions have made the production of that work in its entirety impossible at the present time'. His *Ye Olde Village of Hornchurch*, 'being an illustrated historical handbook of the village and parish of Hornchurch', was finally published in 1917 by Benham and Company of Colchester to meet 'a repeatedly expressed desire . . . for a book on the history of our ancient village'. It is known to many through both its original and reprinted forms – the most recent edition being that published by Ian Henry Publications in 1977 and 1982.

Charles Perfect's wife Nellie had joined the Committee for the Village Nursing Fund in 1908 and the early war years of 1914 saw her and their daughter Dora acting as volunteer workers at the Rest and Social Room. This facility was open each evening in the hall at the rear of the Baptist church in North Street to provide 'rest and quietness, and not less so of the food and refreshment'. Almost certainly Charles Perfect kept careful notes from the early days of war of the local involvement in the conflict. The result is his meticulous record containing a series of detailed descriptions of the various key features locally, with listings of those involved, including a full roll of honour of each parishioner who served 'King and Country'. Perfect's 354-page book *Hornchurch During the Great War*, 'being an illustrated account of local activities and experiences', was published in 1920 within months of the official end of hostilities. Charles' final contribution to Hornchurch's history was his *History of St Andrew's, Hornchurch*, which followed three years later in 1923.

In 1924 towards the end of his long career the sixty-year-old C.T. Perfect was honoured to be appointed as a Member of the Court of the Company of Watermen and Lightermen of the River Thames. In late February 1927 the *Romford Times* reported that Charles had been ill, but by May that year it was able to report that he was now feeling better. However, this recovery was to be short-lived: at the end of August 1927 he was said to be 'lying ill in the Romford Victoria Cottage Hospital. He has undergone an operation and another will be necessary in a few weeks.' This took place at St Thomas' Hospital, London, about three weeks later, and at the same time it was announced that the Perfects would be leaving Hornchurch at the end of February 1928 after twenty-five years in the parish to return to Charles' native Surrey. They were honoured by the parishioners at a social held on 21 February at which they were presented with a grandfather clock and an album bearing a list of subscribers. Earlier the same day the Hornchurch Branch of the Church of England Men's Society, of which Charles Perfect was Chairman, presented him with a 'silver cigarette box suitably inscribed'.

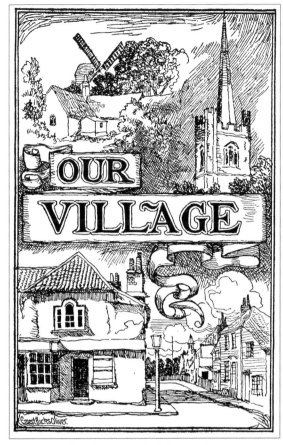

Frontispiece for Charles Perfect's first book *Our Village*.

Charles retired from the Lighterage Department of the Associated Portland Cement Manufacturers Ltd in 1933 after fifty-six years service, and soon afterwards received the accolade of being appointed Master of the Watermen's and Lightermen's Company. In this regard he became the third man with Hornchurch associations to hold this honour, as Mr Thomas Gardner of Dury Falls was Master in 1885 and Mr W. Varco Williams of Langtons held the office in 1905 and 1906.

The Perfects chose Ewell for their retirement and Charles Perfect's last home was Wykeham Lodge, 85 Cheam Road, Ewell. The name of this home evoked memories of Hornchurch for Charles and his wife Ellen, as William of Wykeham, Bishop of Winchester in the fourteenth century, became the owner of estates formerly part of Hornchurch Priory, which were later acquired by New College, Oxford. C.T. Perfect died in Epsom and Ewell Cottage Hospital on 29 November 1939 aged seventy-five due to haemorrhage and duodenal ulcer. His wife Ellen survived him by ten years, dying in 1949.

3. An Industrial Village

Nowadays it is difficult to imagine that in 1876 Hornchurch could be described as a 'large and busy-looking' industrial village. Just yards from the busy High Street the village had a brewery with sixty staff and an innovative iron foundry employing some eighty or ninety hands at its peak.

The Hornchurch Brewery, founded by John Woodfine in 1789, was to the east of Hornchurch village and on the south side of Church Hill. After John Woodfine's death in 1811 his son Thomas (b. 1796) continued and expanded the business, adding buildings nearest to the town centre. After Thomas' premature death in January 1853, aged fifty-six, his son (also named Thomas) became the third generation of the Woodfine family to own the brewery. However, Thomas junior sold the brewery in 1874 and took up farming, firstly at Dury Falls and later at Lea Gardens Farm.

The new owners of the brewery were the Holmes brothers, Benjamin and Henry, who brewed under the name of the Old Hornchurch Brewery. They supplied wines, spirits and aerated waters to four Hornchurch hostelries, as well as thirty or so other houses locally. In August 1883 the brewery was made into a limited company but, as only 200 of the 7,000 available shares were taken up, the company was soon dissolved.

Church Street, looking towards the King's Head. The building on the left is the brewery office.

Charles Dagnall of Horley, Surrey, bought the business from the Holmes brothers in 1889 but his company also met with little success, going into liquidation in December 1890. Philip Conron bought the brewery from the Official Receiver in 1892 and, on his death in 1894, the business was carried on by his sons Philip S. (d. 1897) and Stanislaus R., along with Miss Julia M.M. Percival.

The brewery site ran for 304 feet facing onto Church Hill, and measured 173 feet at its greatest depth. There was a tower brewhouse with three floors, on top of which were the gold-like letters reading 'Hornchurch Brewery', which were visible from a good distance away on a sunny day. The local water supply was said to be particularly suitable for brewing 'bitter' beer. There were three wells, the largest and deepest of them, some 300 feet deep, being sunk in 1910–12 to enable a water supply to be pumped up by means of an engine. Barley was delivered by farmer Thomas Crawford of Suttons Farm into the brewery's two malthouses, and this was malted in kilns sited on the side away from the main road. Brewing took place between twice and four times weekly.

At its peak at the turn of the century the brewery employed some sixty staff, with Mr Goodenough the manager from 1902 to 1920 and Mr F.A. Griffith in charge from 1920 to 1925. Each member of staff was allowed five pints of beer a day, for which they received a brass token which had to be presented at the King's Head opposite. Thirty horses, stabled on the Mill Park side of the brewery, grazed in the meadow between the King's Head and the Council School. Deliveries were only fully mechanised after the First World War.

In 1923 the Hornchurch brewery acquired Fielder's brewery of Brentwood, taking the number of tied houses to over one hundred. Two years later on 3 December 1925 the business, comprising all the brewery buildings and equipment, properties including three cottages adjoining the King's Head, and 23 freehold, 9 leasehold and 6 copyhold licensed houses, was sold to the east London brewers Mann, Crossman and Paulin Ltd for £171,000. Manns had only acquired the business to expand their distribution network of tied houses. The end of the independent Hornchurch Brewery on 31 December 1925 was marked by a farewell dinner, with 'golden handshakes' for the employees.

The brewery remained closed for several years after its take-over; demolition took place between September 1930 and February 1931. The site was sold for development to East Anglian Properties (Maldon) in October 1937 but mostly remained undeveloped until the early 1960s when shops were built there.

Hornchurch's iron industry achieved regional and national renown. According to C.T. Perfect the Wedlake brothers, Thomas and Robert, settled in Hornchurch in 1784 where Thomas is said to have bought Fairkytes in Billet Lane and first the brothers traded as millwrights. The eighteenth-century origins, however, are not supported by the facts. In 1784 the elder brother Thomas was just three years old while Robert was not born and baptised until a few years later in 1789 in Williton. The dating to around 1809 by John Booker, the leading Essex industrial historian, therefore seems more likely than 1784.

Thomas was the head of the firm and the business man while Robert was the mechanic, a perfect combination. The Wedlakes' business concentrated on producing agricultural implements to support the local agricultural economy. The business's success led to a demand for additional hands, which was a key reason for Hornchurch's population growth of over 350 between 1811 and 1821. The foundry's reputation had been established well beyond the local community by 1833 when about seventy 'agricultural gentlemen' from all over Essex and East Anglia presented Thomas Wedlake with a silver tea urn weighing 160 oz as an expression of thanks for his 'inventions and improvements'.

Wedlake's foundry was marked out from others by the degree of originality they showed in exploiting the best uses of cast iron. Thomas Wedlake's ingenuity was an important factor in the foundry's success and for the high regard in which he was held. An article in the Royal Agricultural Society's *Journal* in 1844 referred to him as a 'spirited inventor and improver of agricultural implements'. A price list for the business in 1849 featured eleven kinds of plough, as well as scarifiers, seed-drills, threshing machines and smaller implements such as turnip cutters and pig troughs.

The firm's importance is reflected in the fact that they had an office in Fenchurch Street, another in Billeter Street, and a stand in the New Corn Exchange in Mark Lane. Their market included providing agriculturalists, colonists and emigrants with the tools

The old Foundry Cottage and gates, *c.* 1917.

needed for a new life abroad. The Mark Lane outlet – their 'City of London Repository for Modern Agricultural and Colonial Implements' – had been established by at least 1847 and was quite unique in concept for several years. From the earliest days the company was involved in producing non-agricultural products, in 1829 advertising general castings such as guttering and stove ranges. An early Gothic design milepost by Wedlake, probably dating from around 1820, survives on the north side of Mile End Road at Bow.

Although remnants of the foundry itself have long since disappeared, until well into the current century a visible reminder was the old Foundry Cottage in Billet Lane. This little cottage with its imposing heavy door, described by Perfect in 1917 as 'artistically studded with big nails', served as the foundry office.

On the death in September 1843 of Thomas at the age of sixty-two, the enterprise was continued under the name Mary Wedlake and Co., run by Thomas' widow Mary and her son-in-law Louis Philip De Porquet, husband of Mary's daughter Eliza Mary. After Mary Wedlake herself died in 1846, aged sixty-seven, the De Porquets seem to have continued for a few years. In 1851 the 54-year-old Calais-born Louis De Porquet was living at Fairkytes described as an 'Iron founder and machine maker, author and publisher employing 57 men'. The De Porquets may have quit Hornchurch in 1852 when they sold both Fairkytes and the nearby Little Langtons. By 1855 the Wedlake's Fairkytes Foundry had gone out of business. Thomas' brother Robert had left the foundry by 1848 and had set up a rival business of Wedlake & Thompson at the Union Foundry next to the Bull Inn in the High Street. In 1851 Robert Wedlake, 'Agricultural Implement Maker', and Anne Thompson, 'Iron Founder', were jointly employing thirty-two men at the foundry. Anne was the widow of Charles Thompson, the book-keeper at the Fairkytes Foundry, who had died in February 1845 at the age of forty-nine, leaving Anne to bring up her six surviving children.

Robert Wedlake's daughter Sarah married Richard Dendy in 1852. By 1861, after Robert's retirement, Richard Dendy had taken over the Union Foundry and he was living at Grosvenor House (later known as the White House) in Cage (now North) Street, described as an 'Engineer and founder employing 59 men and 3 boys'. Robert Wedlake died in November 1864, aged seventy-seven, while his widow Sarah passed away seventeen years later in 1881, aged eighty. Wedlake & Dendy, engineers, iron and brass founders, continued the Wedlake association with Hornchurch for many years. The foundry specialised in equipment such as the portable steam machine and thrashing machine exhibited at Halstead Show in 1872.

The partnership between Dendy and Thomas Wedlake ended around 1894. Walter Dendy (b. 1864) took over from his father Richard and transferred the Union Foundry to Barking in 1902 under the name of the London Scottish Foundry. In June 1888 Thomas Wedlake bought a site to the rear of the White House in North Street from a Watson Askew. By 1894 Wedlake had set up the Hornchurch Ironworks, possibly in conjunction with an Edward Shepherd. Assisted by his sons Robert (b. 1872) and

Thomas Wedlake's home, the White House, in North Street.

Wedlake's Cottages, North Street.

Sydney (b. 1876), he continued to trade at the North Street premises as Thomas W. Wedlake & Co., engineers. Thomas died on 21 October 1917, aged eighty-eight, having lived in Hornchurch all his life. Two years later Robert bought the White House and the eight adjacent cottages, together with the foundry and engineering works.

The business continued to be listed as late as 1937, when it seems Robert retired; he died fifteen years later in February 1952. By then the former engineering works site had been sold to Barton Timber Co., which still occupies the site, and in 1956 part of the frontage on North Street was sold to HM Postmaster General to be developed as a telephone exchange. In March 1958 the rest of the premises, including the White House and Wedlake's cottages, was sold by Babette Wedlake, Robert's widow, to Essex County Council for just under £3,000. By 1960 the White House had been demolished and the cottages followed that year, to be replaced by the Hornchurch Branch Library and the Fire Station, built 1964. The Wedlake association is commemorated in Wedlake Close, which runs alongside the library and telephone exchange.

Another industrial business in Hornchurch village was the motor vehicle company later known as Frost Brothers, first established by Jonathan Diaper in the 1850s as a wheelwrights, in premises adjoining the Bull Inn in the High Street. Diaper married Hannah Gates, daughter of Edward Gates, blacksmith in 1844, and their elder daughter,

Frost's new finishing department opened in North Street in 1904. (Chris Saltmarsh)

also Hannah, married the Suffolk-born Charles Frost in the mid-1860s. It seems likely that Frost took over the business after his father-in-law Jonathan Diaper died in 1877. The business developed into building anything on wheels – as well as 'heavy work' carts for market growers and traders their output also included carriages, broughams, gigs, dog-carts and governess carts. With an increasing demand for motor vehicle bodies, and with an eye to the rapid expansion of this side of the work, a new finishing shop was built in North Street in 1904. Vehicles were made in the High Street premises and taken to the finishing works for painting, varnishing, upholstery and trimming. Charles Frost's three sons followed him into the business, which took the name Charles Frost and Sons, specialising in the period between the wars in motor bodies at the North Street works. Following Charles Frost's death the business became Frost Brothers. This location remained as the company's home into the 1970s in the motor sales and car repair trade.

To the west of Hornchurch parish, although more usually associated with Romford, where the River Rom crosses the main west–east route, a cycle works was established by 1890. Initially named the St Andrew's Works it later became the New Ormonde Cycle Works. The Ormonde Cycle Company, whose headquarters were at 79 Wells Street, Oxford Street, was one of the ventures by the millionaire playboy Terence Hooley, whose enterprise soon ended in bankruptcy. For a while the Ramie Fibre Company made gas mantles for home and street lighting from the works and in 1902 the Ormonde Spinning Syndicate, fibre spinners, occupied the premises.

The Neostyle Manufacturing Company Ltd, owned by A.D. Klaber, needed greater capacity than their site at Great Eastern Street in London would allow. In 1906 Klaber discovered the former cycle works and in May 1907 the Neostyle company had taken over the premises in Hornchurch Road. Many of the employees from Great Eastern Street, especially those in the skilled trades, took up jobs at the new office machinery factory. Some settled locally but many travelled daily from Liverpool Street. The company later took the name Roneo Ltd.

The factory had no general works manager. Walter 'Chip' Chipperfield managed the Engineering Section, and Charles Green the Supplies Section, which mainly produced stencils, inks and copier-rolls. The Engineering Section was a self-contained factory. It had a machine shop manned by skilled turners, millers and other hands, a tool room, which produced all the tools needed, and a large iron foundry with its own pattern shop and sand-blasting unit. The works produced its own power at first from a 45 hp gas-driven generator and later two large Mirless engines, which at times fed surplus power into the London Electricity network. At the corner of the site a windmill pumped water from a bore-well for washing and other uses. This became a local landmark known in the works as 'Charlie Green's Amusement Park'. There was also a canteen, originally little more than a kitchen in the yard but later a purpose-built corrugated iron hall near to the gate. The canteen had a dining-room with a stage, frequently used as a club in the evenings, a kitchen and a billiard-room.

A 1910 advertisement for Roneo Limited's office machinery.

4. GREY TOWERS

Grey Towers was perhaps the most photographed building in Hornchurch during the first two decades of this century and it is surprising therefore to record that it was a feature of village life for little more than fifty years.

The story begins in October 1863 with the wedding at St Andrew's, Hornchurch, of Henry Holmes, gent., then living in Walthamstow, and Emilie Helena Mary Wagener, the nineteen-year-old elder daughter of John Wagener, a German-born sugar refiner who lived at Langtons in Billet Lane, Hornchurch. Holmes was the son of John Gilbert

The lodge and the gates through which the Grey Towers Estate was approached.

Holmes, from a leading family of Durham Quakers, originally shipbuilders and ship owners in Middlesbrough. Henry Holmes came south with his father in the mid-1800s and around 1859–60 John Holmes lived at Marshalls in Romford. Henry and Emilie began their married life at Harwood Hall, at Corbets Tey, Upminster, and a large family of five sons and one daughter followed at regular intervals between 1865 and 1875. Added to Henry's extensive family business interest were a directorship of the London, County and Middlesex Bank and in 1874 he became joint proprietor of Old Hornchurch Brewery, with his brother Benjamin.

John Wagener sold some 87 acres of the Langtons Estate to his son-in-law Henry Holmes. In 1876 Holmes built the castellated mansion of Grey Towers in the centre of his new estate as a home for his wife and family. The house was approached through an avenue of lime trees. This entered the estate from Hornchurch Road through two castellated lodges, which reflected the architecture of the house. The park surrounding the new mansion was soon to gain a reputation as the venue for many important local festivities. It was adjoined by terraced gardens leading down to an ornamental lake, created by damming the brook which flowed through the grounds.

Henry Holmes played a full and prominent part in local affairs. In 1882 he raised a Battery of the First Essex Artillery Volunteers, of which he later became colonel, and was henceforth known as Colonel Holmes. He became a JP in 1891 and four years later rose to become chairman of the local bench of magistrates, and he was the first chairman of the Hornchurch School Board in 1889. A staunch Conservative he was for twenty-five years chairman of the Central Council of the Romford Division

Conservative Association. In 1895 he became the first representative of Hornchurch on Essex County Council, later becoming a deputy lieutenant for the County of Essex. Charles Perfect's poem 'The Colonel' captures something of his character:

> Four score and three, his eye not dim,
> Martial in bearing, tall and trim;
> Straight as an arrow, spick and span,
> A fine old English gentleman —
> The Colonel!

Colonel Holmes died on 3 December 1913, aged eighty-five, only a few weeks after celebrating his golden wedding anniversary. Although rather frail, the Colonel had been in good health and his sudden death came as a surprise. His funeral was a grand affair, with all the village shops and businesses closing during the service and flags flown at half-mast. A long procession carried his remains from Grey Towers, through streets lined by village residents, to his final resting place in a brick-lined grave in St Andrew's churchyard. Colonel Holmes' wife Emilie survived him only a few months, dying on 19 April 1914. On her instructions the contents of Grey Towers were sold by auction towards the end of June.

Not long after the outbreak of war in August 1914 the vacant Grey Towers mansion and parklands were, like many other grand houses, commandeered for military use. From November 1914 to June 1915 Grey Towers was the training camp of the

The castellated and ivy-covered Grey Towers mansion, c. 1915.

Three members of the Sportsman's Battalion clear up a fallen tree after a gale in December 1914.

Sportsman's Battalion (23rd Royal Fusiliers), a battalion which contained many who were adept at some branch of sport, the world of entertainment or the professions, some drawn from the ranks of the wealthy or noble families, all mingling together as private soldiers. The Sportsman's Battalion had been raised by Mrs Cunliffe-Owen, who obtained a special concession from King George V which allowed men much older than normal – up to 45-years-old – to enlist. In the weeks before the battalion's arrival in the village hundreds of workmen had busied themselves, erecting huts at what was considered to be a model camp. The barracks were opened for inspection on 22 October 1914 and the local press reported that 'ideal quarters have been provided, and one might almost describe them as luxurious, no detail having been overlooked where the men's comfort is concerned'. Grey Towers mansion itself was converted to form the officers' quarters. Fifty separate buildings, the majority wooden barracks huts containing thirty beds each, were laid out in named streets on either side of the drive. Other buildings housed a hospital and dispensary, a sergeants' mess, guardroom, and cook house, the whole camp being lit with electricity.

The Sportsmen arrived at Grey Towers on the afternoon of 4 November 1914, after travelling by train from Liverpool Street to Romford, having previously marched through London, from Hyde Park to the City, through crowds of people lining the streets, before being addressed at the Mansion House by the Lord Mayor. Their welcome at Hornchurch was in similar fashion, with the band of the Cottage Homes heading the procession as they marched through the entrance gates for the first time. Over the coming winter months the Sportsmen played a hearty part in village life. A Rest Room was opened in North Street in the schoolroom in the rear of the Baptist

Funeral procession escorted by members of the Sportsman's Battalion, 1915.

church, which was packed each night with soldiers from the camp. Many social events, dances and concerts also contributed to the close relationship between the camp and village folk and columns of soldiers marching or on an early morning run became a familiar sight. They also displayed their undoubted sporting prowess in a series of football fixtures and were starting to make a good start at cricket when their season came to an abrupt end with the news of their transfer from the camp. Their departure came on the morning of 26 June 1915 when, despite the early hour, the streets of the village on the route to Hornchurch Station were lined by a mass of villagers. The battalion departed for Clipstone Camp to finish training, and transferred to France in November that year.

For the next few months Grey Towers Camp remained empty until, in November 1915, the 26th Battalion Middlesex Regiment (known universally as the Navvies' or Pioneers' Battalion) took up residence. As its name implies, this battalion was recruited largely to carry out manual work needed to support the military effort. Its stay was short for just before Christmas the men received their orders to vacate their billet and on 21 December 1915 they marched out of Grey Towers for the railway station, en route to their next camp.

The forces against Germany and its allies not only comprised British servicemen but also regular drafts from Canada, India, Australia, New Zealand, South Africa as well as other dominions and dependencies. In 1915 the Australians and New Zealanders were engaged in the bloody and largely futile campaign on the Gallipoli Peninsula in Turkey

Departure of the Sportsman's Battalion, Station Lane, 26 June 1915. (Christine Halsall)

and large numbers of wounded were sent to Britain for treatment and convalescence. A convalescent hospital was set up at Epsom, Surrey, and from January 1916 New Zealanders treated there were sent on to the Hornchurch Grey Towers camp as convalescents. Grey Towers initially became the Command Depot from which servicemen were despatched to their respective units. The rows of huts established for the Sportsman's Battalion became home to the New Zealanders, whose distinctive slouch hats were soon a familiar sight in the streets of Hornchurch. From March 1916 a branch of the New Zealanders' club was opened in Hornchurch, with a reading and writing room, and a small buffet, which could only accommodate fifteen to twenty men at a time. The following month a more spacious 'hut' was opened at a house in Butts Green Road, Hornchurch, renamed 'Te Whare Puni' – 'The Meeting Place' – and equipped with a full-sized billiard table, piano and gramophone, with a tennis court nearby. Financed by private individuals, mainly New Zealanders, the club was supported by voluntary efforts of ladies, and food was supplied at a low charge to cover materials costs only.

When the New Zealanders joined the European war in late April/early May 1916, the flow of wounded and sick reaching England increased dramatically and it was realised that a convalescent hospital needed to be established at Grey Towers. In July 1916 the bulk of the 'details' at Grey Towers were transferred to Salisbury Plain and the Convalescent Hospital was set up. Two months later in September 1916 the camp came under the command of a medical officer, rather than a combatant officer. A great deal of remodelling was needed to change the site from a battalion training camp to a medical facility. An up-to-date surgical department was formed and a well-equipped gymnasium was set up and quickly became one of the most important features of the New Zealanders' hospital. Men attended half hourly sessions under an expert instructor and his trained staff. The object was to restore men to fitness so that they could return to their fighting unit in France. If this was not possible after around six months, they went home to New Zealand by ship; the voyage often proved to be a suitable convalescence in itself, and many were later transported back to the Western Front.

The Grey Towers hospital was at first intended to accommodate 1,500 patients, but this soon proved inadequate and was raised to 2,000 and again to 2,500. It was essential to find some useful occupation for so many men. At the expense of the New Zealand War Contingent Association a large hut was built containing a canteen, a large hall, a billiard-room, and reading and writing rooms and staffed primarily by New Zealand ladies, with some local help. The New Zealand YMCA also established a large hut at Grey Towers, which was extended several times. This block consisted of a canteen, a large hall capable of seating 800 to 900 people, a workshop, initially known as the arts and crafts department, and a large reading and writing room. Mr Horace Fawcett, local secretary of the New Zealand YMCA, was appointed as director, supported by a medical officer. Every evening entertainments of some kind were arranged in one of the two recreation halls, and a cinema was installed in the YMCA

The YMCA hut, Grey Towers, 1917, with Horace Fawcett, Secretary and later Director of the local YMCA, standing centre front.

New Zealand servicemen relaxing around the Drive, one of the main routes through Grey Towers Camp, 1917.

hut. Sporting teams were formed and a swimming bath was built in the stream at the west of the camp. Many dances were held at Grey Towers, to which Hornchurch folk were invited, and several large scale entertainments were given in the Drill Hall in Hornchurch village, some in aid of local charities.

From early 1918 an extensive educational scheme was put into effect to assist with the demobilisation of troops and their employment at the end of the war. The aim was to train men as expert workers in many fields, so that on return to New Zealand they could find a job. On 6 December 1918 an addition to the YMCA hut was opened in this connection, comprising an education office, workshops and classrooms and serving as the headquarters of the New Zealanders' educational work in England. By the end of 1918, once hostilities had ended, some 20,000 men were reckoned to have passed through the convalescent hospital. In the early months of 1919 the west part of Grey Towers took over from Watford as No.2 Transfer Centre, which reassigned troops to units where they were better suited, and it also became the main unit carrying out the work of demobilisation. From this time Grey Towers house was no longer used by the camp. All the New Zealanders were finally evacuated from Grey Towers in June 1919 and Hornchurch returned to being a peace-time village. One of the few remaining uses of Grey Towers, post-war, was as a venue for scout, guide and brownie camps. In October 1922 Grey Towers and its 87-acre estate were sold to Mrs Elizabeth Parkes of Langtons, reuniting the original Langtons Estate out of which Grey Towers had been created fifty years before.

5. EMERSON PARK

Towards the end of June 1895 an advertisement in the *Essex Weekly News* drew attention to the impending sale by auction on 4 July 1895 of sixty plots of freehold building land on the proposed Emerson Park Estate. The sale catalogue claimed that the 'estate undoubtedly occupies the best position in this healthy village' and that plots had 'good depths allowing for spacious gardens and can be well adapted for the erection of private residences'. Buyers from London could take advantage of 'a limited number of free rail tickets . . . from Fenchurch Street Station', with luncheon provided at 1.30 p.m. in a marquee on the estate. Roads were already being laid out and the original plans showed the estate divided into some 193 plots, of which only 60 were offered for sale initially. A large site to the west of Nelmes Road and south of Parkstone Avenue was reserved for a recreation ground and cycle track, although this was soon to be developed as Berther Road, which ran eastwards to Nelmes Road.

The new Emerson Park Estate was on the southern part of the historic manor of Nelmes, comprising some 200 acres lying north of the recently opened railway from Romford to Grays, bounded on the west by 'Station Road', now known as Butts Green Road, and Wingletye Road (now Lane) to the east, together with 20 acres of the manor

The manor house of Nelmes.

of Lees Gardens. The manor of Nelmes had in earlier times been known as Elms, taking its name from the family of Elms (de Ulmis) who were prominent locally in the thirteenth and fourteenth centuries. Over the years it changed hands many times, and the estate had been bought in 1781 by trustees of the will of Richard Newman, apparently acting on behalf of Newman's nephew and heir, Richard Harding, who later took the name Newman. It remained in the possession of the Newman family and it was Benjamin H. Newman who sold the southern part of the estate in 1895.

The estate developer was William Carter of Parkstone, Dorset, and the estate was named after his eldest son, Emerson (b. 1878). Roads on the estate took their names from his other children: Herbert Road was named after Carter's second son, Herbert (b. 1880); Ernest Road was probably named after Charles Ernest Owen (b. 1887); while Isabel Road (later renamed Burntwood Avenue) may have been so called after Mary Annie Isobel, who died as a baby in that year. This followed Carter's practice in other developments. In Poole, for instance, he had also named two roads after his elder sons Emerson and Herbert. Carter Road (now Maybush Road) took its name from the estate owner, while Parkstone Avenue, the principal route across the initial development, was named after Carter's adopted home town. Of the roads identified on the original plans, only Nelmes Road – named after the manor – did not have a personal connection with Carter.

William and Eliza Carter, with their sons Emerson, Charles and Herbert. (Tony Carter)

William Carter had served no formal apprenticeship in the building trade but was, according to his son Herbert, 'a capable worker with hands as well as brain and made substantial if erratic progress'. Born at Winchester in 1852, the second son of Jesse Carter (1830–1927), a tile maker, and Mary Callaway, he bought in 1884 the ailing Kinson Pottery in Parkstone, Dorset, teaching himself the pottery trade and putting the business on a sound footing and expanding the trade. He also broadened his interests to cover land purchase, speculative house building and buying bankrupt businesses.

The growing Carter family moved into the mud-walled cottage known as the Hermitage, located on the southern side of the Pottery site on Parkstone Heights, a spur with magnificent views over Poole Harbour, the Purbeck Hills and much of Dorset. The Hermitage was progressively extended by adding a new dining-room, a new kitchen, raising the roof and adding three new bedrooms. The further addition in 1928 of a castellated observation tower ensured that the surrounding pine trees did not obstruct the magnificent view. The tower housed Carter's reflector telescope which, it was said, was used to keep under constant observation his employees at the Hamworthy Junction Brickworks, which he later bought!

William Carter's son Herbert later described the distinguishing feature of his father as his extreme friendliness. He was also a confirmed globe-trotter, and trips to Switzerland gave him the idea of founding a travelling club, as a result of which he and his wife would take charge of touring parties. Any profits were used to offer cheap fares that allowed many to afford a trip which would otherwise have remained out of reach. Annual reunions of travellers were held in London, at which plans for the next year's activities were laid. Carter was also an accomplished cyclist, even taking part in races.

But despite these wide-ranging interests, in the words of his son, William Carter's main hobby remained 'money-making', but with a purpose: 'the purchase of land and houses, the laying out of estates, and the settling of city-dwellers amid rural surroundings.' In this regard, Carter's friendship with Ebenezer Howard, the originator in England of the 'Garden City' concept brought to public attention in the 1898 book *Garden Cities of Tomorrow*, was an obvious influence, as no doubt were his visits to William Lever, later Lord Leverhulme, who laid out Port Sunlight as a model town for his employees.

William Carter's initial ventures into estate development seem to have been in his home town of Poole, and later in around 1880 at Woking, where his son Emerson was born that year. In addition to developing the 220-acre Emerson Park Estate in Hornchurch, by the early years of this century Carter's other major developments included the 131-acre Medstead estate, near Winchester, the 300-acre Beech Place Estate at Alton, Hampshire and a 200-acre development at Andover. He also developed the town of Carterton, near Brize Norton, Oxfordshire, in 1900.

Carter's main local agent for the Emerson Park Estate was William Horner Cowley Curtis, who made his home in Glenroy, one of the first houses built in Berther Road. It can surely be no coincidence that Curtis was born in Poole, Dorset, in 1858. His original trade was a house carpenter and it seems likely that Carter and Curtis became acquainted through business associations in Poole, and that this relationship continued as Carter extended his activities further afield.

The auction of plots in a marquee in July 1895 on the Nelmes Estate saw the first lots knocked down at prices ranging from £85 to £145 to buyers from the Manor Park or the Hornchurch areas. The original plans show that Emerson Park was not to be a speculative development, as plots ranged from ½ an acre up to 2 acres in extent, with an average of 1 acre. Purchasers could either engage their own builders or use the services of Carter's company, later known as Homesteads Ltd, which offered a selection of houses and bungalows built to a range of individualistic designs. Building costs seem to have ranged from below £400 to over £1,500 for the largest of the detached designs. Some purchasers chose not to build on their plots for several years.

The first properties at Emerson Park had been occupied by June 1897 and building work progressed rapidly across the whole of the planned estate over the next few years. By early 1899 the plans had changed and the development of smaller bungalows in Berther Road had replaced the original plans for a recreation ground. To the south-east of the estate the plans were amended to take in a bungalow development of Curtis Road (named after Curtis the site agent), Poole Road (after Curtis' and Carter's Dorset connections), as well as housing on the adjacent stretch of Wingletye Lane. In contrast to the original part of Emerson Park, these properties seem to have been speculatively built by the developer for sale. By February 1901, 109 houses had been built or started on Emerson Park, including 31 on Parkstone Avenue, 19 on Herbert Road, 17 on Curtis Road (with 18 further sanctioned), 15 on Berther Road and 10 on Carter Road.

Shops on Butts Green Road, opposite Berther Road, Emerson Park.

Housing on a still rural Wingletye Lane, *c.* 1906.

Although the early occupiers on the estate seem to have been satisfied with their purchases – if the testimonials printed in Carter's later catalogue can be believed – life on the new estate was not without its problems. Houses were not initially linked to mains drainage, each having a cesspool, and Romford Rural District Council only brought forward plans for sewers in March 1899. For the first few years there was no refuse collection service, the council taking the view that the estate was not 'sufficiently developed' and that the refuse could be 'utilized to advantage' on the large gardens.

In May 1901 the Newman family offered for sale a further 241 acres of the Nelmes Park Estate, including Little Nelmes dairy farm which was leased to Mr Banyard until September 1904. The location was directly to the north of the Emerson Park Estate and Nelmes was said to be 'undoubtedly exceedingly valuable as a building estate'. The purchaser was Alfred Barber who had lived in Hornchurch since 1894 and had already developed estates elsewhere in Essex. He took up residence in Nelmes Manor House and 10 acres surrounding, and developed plans for the remainder, to be known as the Great Nelmes Estate. As the sale catalogue, issued in April 1904, indicated the estate was 'being developed to suit the needs of the middle classes who can reside in a house of a rental from £30 to £60 per annum'. A later prospectus described Great Nelmes as 'a really rural retreat for the City man within 14 miles of his work and within this distance of town it would be difficult to find a spot so sequested and so beautifully wooded'. As the 1904 catalogue stated 'no tree will be unnecessarily disturbed and every effort will be made to retain the rural and park like appearance of the estate and as much variety as possible will be introduced. The object will be to avoid any impression of a monotonous suburban building estate.' Plots had at least 60 feet of road frontage and most were 300 feet deep. All buildings were to be of good design and no semi-detached or terraced houses were to be allowed.

Woodlands Avenue, Great Nelmes Estate.

Woodlands Avenue and Elm Grove had already been laid out by 1904, and Sylvan Avenue was to follow. Elm Grove retained a 'double row of magnificent elms of mature growth' while Woodlands Avenue was cut through a pine wood and Sylvan Avenue was said to open up 'a most attractive section of the park'. Roads were described as 'of exceptional width' and rolled by steam rollers, with granite kerbs and wide paths (this was in contrast to the early experiences of Emerson Park residents who found some of their roads impassable for many years).

The third phase of development of the area came after the First World War when farmers and land owners increasingly decided to sell their holdings and developers were able to buy land at reasonable prices. This expansion of the estate was by E.A. Coryn and Son, developing northwards between Woodlands Avenue, with Ardleigh Green Road on the west and Nelmes Way to the east. From the early 1930s Coryn built character houses on the Great Nelmes Estate and one of the first houses to be completed was Allen Coryn's own house on the corner of Ardleigh Green Road and Ayloffs Walk. Unlike much of the development elsewhere in Hornchurch which was speculative, houses developed by the company on the Great Nelmes Estate were individually architect designed for the purchasers, who had been subject to 'vetting' by Allen Coryn himself. Houses sold at that time for between £800 and £1,000 and there was a series of restrictive clauses in the deeds aimed at preserving the character of the estate by preventing unwanted developments, including garden sheds. The Coryn family encouraged a community atmosphere, including a summer fête and flower show, held in a marquee in a field at the corner of Slewins Lane next to their estate office, and a bonfire party in November, which was still held into the 1940s. After Allen Coryn moved away from the area in 1944 he had much less direct involvement, and most design work was handled by Harry Macaree. The company carried on for a few years after Allen Coryn's death in 1963 but it was then wound up.

Further developments to Emerson Park and Great Nelmes have continued since the Second World War. The roads in the area between Nelmes Crescent, Sylvan Avenue and Wingletye Lane were developed by the firm of Thomas Bates. Percy Bates had lived in Nelmes Crescent before moving to Capel Nelmes in the 1950s. This house was formerly the stables, groom's quarters and what is believed to have been the chapel of Nelmes Manor. Before the land was built over, the Bates' family held a popular annual gymkhana on fields adjoining the Chase in Nelmes Crescent.

Nelmes Manor House was a sixteenth-century house which had a magnificent (seventeenth-century) carved staircase and contemporary panelling. The year after the last occupier, John Platford, died in 1966 this fine listed building was illegally demolished by his heir before the local council could intervene. The land was later sold to Luck Brothers who built the close of houses called the Witherings, named after Thomas Withering (d. 1651), Postmaster General to Charles I who had lived in Nelmes Manor House. The final large-scale development came with the sale of the Little Nelmes Farm and its lands by the Banyard family. Despite considerable local opposition planning permission was finally granted and in 1979 Luck Brothers started the Nelmes Park Estate, which retains as a feature the adjacent 10-acre landscaped park and lake.

6. HOUSING DEVELOPMENT
BEFORE 1925

Romford had grown rapidly after the opening of the railway service in 1839 gave it a fast rail route to London. It is perhaps not surprising that the further opening up – by the London, Tilbury and Southend rail extension running eastwards from Barking to Pitsea – of a part of the Essex countryside 'hitherto almost unknown to the London holiday maker' should be heralded as the key to the development of the district. On 12 October 1883, the day after the ceremonial cutting of the turf which set work on this line underway, the *Daily Telegraph* urged that those who wished to see Hornchurch 'as it is, and as it has been for centuries, must visit it soon', as the new railway would 'bring the place within half an hour of London, and open up a new field for the speculative contractor'. But in many ways this prediction

A London-bound train passing through Hornchurch Station.

was wide of the mark. Although the large-scale development of Nelmes Manor as the Emerson Park Estate was well underway before the century closed, the development of much of Hornchurch, particularly the area around the ancient village, had to wait for several decades. One reason for this was that large parts of Hornchurch were in a limited number of hands, in particular, New College, Oxford, whose landownership in the parish had been recorded as 930 acres in 1849, including Suttons (406 acres) and Hornchurch Hall (280 acres). In addition, the Newman family's Nelmes Estate comprised some 573 acres.

But had the author of the *Daily Telegraph* article done his homework, he would have found signs of the first urban stirrings in Hornchurch's otherwise rural landscape. More than twenty years before, the fast-developing Romford had spread across the ill-defined parish boundary into Hornchurch. Housing developments made their impact on this part of north-west Hornchurch in the late 1860s after 'The Romford Estate' of 60 acres was sold in 1860. By 1881 a small estate, referred to in 1873 as 'New Hornchurch', had sprung up around the western end of Brentwood Road, with housing already established on the west side of Kyme and the south side of Dymoke Roads and at Oak Terrace on Hornchurch Road. Further east along Brentwood Road the southward development of Globe Road, known as the Rosemount Estate, had begun. By 1881 the population of the parish had reached 2,824, a modest rise of around 250 over the 1871 count and still a fairly small increase of 600 over the 1861 total of 2,227.

But in the last two decades of the nineteenth century, particularly during the 1890s, the population increase accelerated. By 1901 the total had more than doubled to 6,402, although part of this increase was accounted for by the new Hornchurch Cottage

Homes, with 297 resident children and 38 staff and their families. The Emerson Park Estate was well underway while in north-west Hornchurch significant further developments had also occurred. The Ordnance Survey map of 1897 confirms that building had taken place on Brentwood Road between Park Lane and Globe Road, with housing in Claremont Road also well established. Building was underway in Clifton and Malvern Roads, while Douglas and Craigdale Roads had also been laid out ready for development by 1897.

Much of the development in the Brentwood Road area had been carried out by the Hunnable brothers, George and William. Originally from Braintree, they settled in Romford and contributed much to the growth of Romford and north-west Hornchurch from the mid-1890s. William Hunnable, who died in 1928 aged sixty-nine, was a leading member of the Romford Urban Council, later buying and developing the large Marshalls Park Estate.

The local population in north-west Hornchurch was provided with new shops as well as housing but, as in many estates, the roads were not properly made up and sewers were not laid for some years. The Medical Officer for Health reported in April 1899 that 'this locality is now being thickly populated and the present sanitary arrangements are very inadequate'. In November 1899 eighty-seven residents in Globe, Claremont, Clifton, Malvern and Douglas Roads and Park Lane petitioned the Rural Council for their roads to be made up. This work seems to have taken place the next year.

Looking east down Brentwood Road. The junction with Globe Road is on the left.

Hornchurch Road, now South Street.

Hornchurch Road (now South Street) was the focus for a number of substantially built, four-bedroomed semi-detached houses from 1901 onwards. To the east along Brentwood Road a small development of villas and distinctive houses was built in the 1890s on part of Great Gardens Farm, running parallel to the southern side of the branch line from Romford to Grays, which had opened in 1893. This was the beginnings of Osborne Road, developed on the estate of Osborne Samuel Delgano Osborne, whose name it presumably took. Further development in north-west Hornchurch came in 1900 with the Longfield Estate, to the east of Hornchurch Road and north of the new Clydesdale Road, built by Ernest J. Little, architect and surveyor of Kilarney, Brentwood Road. He was the son of John Little, of Hylands, Brentwood Road, and between 1896 and 1899 E.J. Little bought around 24 acres of land from O.S.D. Osborne with the intention of developing the Hylands Estate. This development site on Globe Road, which no doubt took its name from his father's house or some other family connection, remained essentially undeveloped on its owner's death in 1911 and later became Hylands Park.

The early years of the twentieth century brought the first tentative housing developments around Hornchurch village. From around 1898 building had begun at the Hornchurch end of Station Lane, with the laying out of two roads, probably The Avenue and Stanley Road, by Joseph Turner, with Devonshire Road developed within a couple of years. Several large detached and semi-detached houses, many still surviving, were also erected on either side of Station Lane, including the home of Hornchurch's

Terraced houses on the west side of Station Lane, built around 1902.

historian, Charles Perfect, who bought the newly built Weylands and the adjacent Woodstock in 1902. On the eastern side of Station Lane the first housing on Mill Park Avenue and Mavis Grove had been developed by the Hornchurch Real Estate Company, one of whose directors was Robert Living, next door neighbour to Charles Perfect. Closer to the village on the west side of Station Lane a terrace of twelve cottages was built in 1902; initially owned by another of the Hunnable brothers, Walter, and a Mr A. Hill, they are now all converted to shops or restaurants. To the west of the village, on the approaches from the Abbs Cross Lane junction, terraces and semi-detached housing were also built at the start of the century, with George Franklyn's terraced Parkside Cottages, and Chenies Villas (Catchpole), Bedford Villas (Bratchell) and Fairview and Parkside (Dockrill), all built by local businessmen. North of the village small-scale housing developments were added on North Street and at Butts Green, close by the Chequers Inn, while to the west, close to the Harrow Inn, came the development of Harrow Drive.

The scale of the new housing in Hornchurch is reflected in the population increase from 1901 to 1911, rising almost by half from 6,402 to 9,462. Much of this was because of the rapid growth of Emerson Park and the northern extension of Great Nelmes. The decade from 1911 to 1921 was dominated by the First World War, which for obvious reasons virtually put an end to house building activities. By 1921 the population of Hornchurch had increased by less than 1,500, reaching 10,891. One new estate at this time, however, was the Walden Estate, situated off Butts Green Road, to the west of Emerson Park, started by the builder Edgar Coryn in 1912. Walden Road had been developed by 1914 with large detached and semi-detached houses, on spacious plots. Similar, but more limited, development had started on Wykeham Avenue, Walden Way and Fanshawe Crescent.

Coryn himself lived at this time at Walden in Walden Way and his son, Herbert Allen (known as Allen), who joined his father in the business in 1919, later lived in the same road at Welwyn, this house taking its name from Welwyn Garden City where Allen Coryn had worked as clerk of works after qualifying as an architect from Regent Street Polytechnic. Both houses were built using bricks made in the brickfield opposite. The estate became rather notorious – fifteen years later the roads still remained as unmade grass tracks. The firm of E.A. Coryn and Sons moved on to develop the Haynes Park Estate, including Haynes Road, which was already underway by 1927. The former Haynes Park Road was renamed Ardleigh Green Road and development of the Great Nelmes Estate by the company followed.

The lack of house building during the war years resulted in a shortage of homes in the years that followed. Just as the world had changed during the war so too had the prospects and returns for potential landlords, who no longer found investing in property 'as safe as houses', as it had been in earlier years. And the shortage of labour

Housing in Walden Road on the new Walden Estate, developed in the first decade of this century. The estate office is on the right.

Bungalows on Haynes Park Road.

as well as materials made it costly and difficult for developers to resume house building and to realise the government's promise of 'homes fit for heroes'. It was against this background that the government introduced for the first time generous state incentives under the Addison Act of 1919 to allow councils to build houses, with subsidies for private builders putting up cheaper housing for rent or purchase. From 1923 a system allowing local councils to offer mortgages on lower priced housing, or guarantee payments to building societies, effectively replaced support for council housing.

Such was the shortage of housing locally that in January 1920 negotiations with the Army led to some of the huts from Grey Towers camp being converted to residential use. Two sites in Hornchurch parish were opened, on Longfield Road in north-west Hornchurch and in South Hornchurch on Rainham Road: these were known as The Hutments.

During the early 1920s, in the five years including 1925, around 650 houses were built in Hornchurch, with the peak years being 1922 with 158 completions followed by 1925 with 213. The parish council estimated in 1925 that the population had risen to 13,800 in that year, an increase of 3,000 in the four years since 1921, with an expected population of 20,000 in five years and 35,000 in ten years. However, it is probable that the 1925 figure, based on five people in each new household, was an overestimation, as the size of the average household and family was falling, particularly in the new home-owning middle classes.

7. HOUSING FROM 1925 ONWARDS

Despite the growth in population before 1925, vast areas of the parish remained undeveloped and were still farmland. But from 1925 onwards more landowners gave up the struggle to make a profitable income from the depressed agricultural market and decided to sell their holdings for development. Land became relatively cheap and this encouraged speculative builders to buy land and develop it for housing. From 1925 to the early 1930s the pace of development expanded considerably and Hornchurch became less rural and progressively more urban. In 1926 the Medical Officer of Health was already able to report that 'owing to the rapid development of building estates the district was now becoming residential in character and was attracting persons whose occupations lay in or near London'.

In 1925 the main road west out of Hornchurch village was still almost completely rural and was virtually free of any housing from the entrance to Grey Towers to the parish border with Romford and Dagenham near the River Rom at Haveringwell hamlet. The only exception was the small estate of Harrow Drive. The whole of the area immediately to the south of Hornchurch Road comprised three farms – Haveringwell Farm (73 acres), Coxes Farm (106 acres) and Maylands Green Farm (167 acres) – all by 1920 in the ownership of Alfred Reeve Gay of Coxes Farm and his

Shops being developed on Hornchurch Road, looking east towards the LGOC Bus garage.

Shops at Grenfell Corner, on the Haveringwell Estate.

brother John Turner Gay of Brentwood Road. Within a decade this whole area had been considerably developed and by the outbreak of war was virtually complete.

The first development was the 30-acre Kingswood Estate laid out to the south of the Hornchurch Road, on part of Coxes Farm between Coxes Farmhouse and the recently built London General Omnibus Company's bus garage by the major developer Allen Ansell in summer 1926. The estate plan, comprising four roads – Dorian, Babington, Candover and Vicarage Roads – provided for one road (Dorian) to run up to the western boundary of the estate, so that it could be extended onto adjoining lands when necessary.

Further west, and also to the south of the main Hornchurch to Dagenham Road, opposite the Crown Inn, Thomas England developed Haveringwell Farm to form the estate of the same name. The layout was approved in January 1927 and development initially concentrated southwards down Rainham Road and roads leading off it. England was a major local figure, later described by Glyn Richards, former editor of the *Romford Recorder* and first public relations officer of the London Borough of Havering, as 'a visionary . . . [who] could anticipate events and developments' and as 'an outstanding character in the community life of Romford'. Chairman of the Romford Urban District Council in the early 1920s, England was actively involved in the setting up of a YMCA in the area, initially in North Street. It was through his generosity that the present YMCA site on part of the Haveringwell Estate was acquired. As well as England, several builders were active on the estate including Thomas Clark and A. Oldreive (both

Rainsford Way), M. Soulsby (Hayburn Way), and G. Crabb (Edison Avenue), typically building blocks of between four and twelve houses or bungalows every two or three months.

To the north of the Hornchurch Road and to the east of Park Lane, William Jackson's former Bush Elms Farm was developed as the Bush Elms Estate by A.J. Carter from early 1929. This estate, mainly of terraced and semi-detached houses, spread northwards to join with the older Rosemount Estate around Globe Road, which was still being extended in 1925. The lengthy Hillcrest Road, mainly built from June 1929 onwards, crossed the estate from west to east. To the west and south of the Bush Elms development, the northern part of Coxes Farm was developed to form North Down, South Down, Cheviot and Purbeck Roads.

The first stirrings in the development of the area between Hornchurch Station and the town centre came in April 1925 when the Hornchurch Development Company's plans for the layout of the Suttons Manor Estate were approved, the company offering to meet half the costs of dealing with sewerage and surface water. This development was on Station Lane and what was then called Blind Lane, which ran westwards between Station Lane and Abbs Cross Lane. Blind Lane was to be replaced by a new, straighter road – Suttons Avenue – which joined Station Lane further north, while the former eastern end of Blind Lane was renamed Suttons Gardens in 1927. Development of this estate, and roads running off Suttons Gardens, was in full swing in 1928 and 1929. By Autumn 1930 around 200 houses had been built in Suttons Avenue alone, with 50 in Wayside Way and 40 on Urban Avenue.

Housing on Station Lane in the late 1920s, soon after they were built. The main road is still unmade.

David Standen and sons. Back row, left to right: Albert, Frederick, Harold, Jack; front row: Charlie, David J., and Frank. (Derek Standen)

By this time the bulk of the eligible Suttons Farm had been sold to the Air Ministry by New College, Oxford, who opened a new airfield on 1 April 1928. The first major housing development on the farm only came after 1930, when land to the east of Station Lane was sold to Mrs Winifred J. Standen, who developed the Station Estate. Over the next few years the Standen family, particularly Mrs Standen's stepson Mr Frederick E. Standen, were to have a troubled relationship with the newly established Urban District Council. The company had been established by David J. Standen, builder and decorator of Southend, but after his bankruptcy in 1926, his second wife Winifred continued the business, with her husband as manager. They first came to Hornchurch in 1927. Frederick had worked for his father but he and his brother Albert traded as Standen Brothers, at first at Hockley but from 1928 onwards building actively in Hornchurch to the north of the railway on the Slewins Lane Estate, in particular in Hazelmere Gardens, Hillview Avenue, Warrington Road (odd numbers) and Brooklands Gardens (even numbers). Mrs Standen developed south of the railway while her stepsons kept to the north side although there were exceptions, Mrs Standen building bungalows at Minster Way from 1928. The Minster Way development was the subject of a court case in 1934 when Mrs Standen unsuccessfully claimed that W.T. Lamb and Sons, brickmakers, had supplied defective bricks used in bungalows in this estate (Nos 2, 4, 6 and 8 Minster Way), one of which had partly collapsed. It was clearly established that the bricks had been sold to her as sub-standard, not suitable for building, and she lost her claim. There was also a long-running dispute over the levying of cesspool emptying rates on the Standens' Station Estate, as before the properties had been joined to the main sewer adequate arrangements for emptying the cesspools had not been put in place.

The year 1933 saw an extraordinary series of public disagreements. In 1932, after several unsuccessful attempts, Frederick Standen had gained election to the Urban Council, and according to the *Romford Times* was 'determined to cause some flutterings in the Council dovecote'. Almost immediately he led an attack on the council's decision to give the clerk, Mr Allen, a £100 honorarium and in 1933 was again the focus of 'extraordinary scenes', which culminated in him striking another councillor and being barred by the council from attending committee meetings, and almost being ejected from a council meeting for not obeying the chair. This led to him launching four writs against the clerk to the council, the chairman, another councillor and against the *Romford Recorder*. The claim against the local paper and its editor, Glyn Richards, came to court in April 1934. Standen claimed that he had been libelled in March 1933 when the newspaper printed a letter alleging that he had used his position as a councillor for personal gain. After a three and a half day hearing the jury found against Standen, awarding damages to the newspaper. Mr Standen's council career was short-lived and the following month he resigned his seat. His career as a developer was also nearing its end. In the autumn of 1934 he was declared bankrupt, following in the footsteps of both his father and grandfather, the costs awarded against him from the unsuccessful libel cases, together with losses from house building and forced sales contributing to his demise.

In South Hornchurch a major development was launched in September 1925 when plans for the Great Mardyke Estate of 1,215 houses on 103 acres were approved, a density of over 12 houses per acre. This estate was built on the former Mardyke Farm, part of the manor of the same name that lay on the edge of the Thames marshes. The estate's origins can be traced to the early thirteenth century when a piece of land held by Gillian, daughter of Ellis, was carried in marriage to William of Mardyke. Mardyke was a house of some importance at the end of the sixteenth century, when it was the seat of Sir Sebastian Harvey, ironmonger and Lord Mayor of London (d. 1621).

Plans for developments on the much smaller Whybridge Estate in South Hornchurch, initially of fifty-nine houses on 8 acres, were also put forward for approval in September 1925. This estate was developed to form Betterton, Hubert, Edmund, Manser Roads, etc. The manor and farm of Whybridge, which lay to the east of Mardyke, had extended to 312 acres in 1849. It probably took its name from the Whybridge family, who held several tenements in Hornchurch in the thirteenth and fourteenth centuries. In the fifteenth century it took the second name of Rands, after it was bought in 1455 by one John Rand, and the manor was usually known then as Whybridge and Rands. The development of this estate, however, was a source of some difficulty for the Hornchurch UDC after it took over in 1926. Unlike most estates, Whybridge was sold off in a piecemeal fashion, mainly in individual plots. Although many purchasers built decent houses, many other properties were mere shacks or hovels, scarcely fit for habitation. There was no mains water and no sewage facilities

Shopping Parade on South End Road, opposite the Cherry Tree, South Hornchurch.

and some houses were served by a well from which the water drawn was unfit for human consumption. Another major development in South Hornchurch came in 1937 when Smith & Black, estate developers of Rainham, purchased the 69½-acre Dovers Farm for £35,500. This estate fronting on New Road, on South End Road and along Cherry Tree Lane was ripe for development and was claimed to be 'one of the last pieces of land of its type available for many miles around'.

By August 1930, 3,500 houses had been built since the setting up of the Hornchurch Urban District in April 1926, with almost 1,200 houses completed in 1929 alone, while a further 1,600 were at that time under construction. More were to come, and the further release of land held by New College, Oxford, was a key factor.

In July 1930 New College offered for sale the 38½ acres of land around Hornchurch Hall Farm. This was described in the sale catalogue as a block of 'ripe building land . . . [which] forms one of the choicest building estates in this rapidly growing district'. Along with Suttons, the manor of Hornchurch Hall formed part of the original endowment of Hornchurch Priory made by Henry II. The rectorial glebe around the church became the nucleus of the manor of Hornchurch Hall, and in 1663 comprised some 184 acres of the overall 306-acre estate. The hall itself was known in the sixteenth century as The Rectory and had probably been part of Hornchurch Priory. In 1923 it was described as a sixteenth-century house with a seventeenth-century chimney, while it is likely that the south front dated from the late eighteenth, or early nineteenth, century. In 1930 the house was occupied on a lease of twenty-one years or her lifetime by the widow of Mr John Gill, who had farmed the Hall Estate for many years. This estate, opposite St Andrew's church and covering much of the area between North

Street and Wingletye Lane, was developed in the 1930s by the British Land Co. and Robert Beard.

Robert Beard had become an increasingly prominent figure in Hornchurch throughout the 1930s. Born in Dagenham, where he traded in the family baker's and confectioner's business, he came to Hornchurch around 1910 and opened a similar shop in the High Street, later expanding the business with shops in Romford and Rainham. He played an active part in the community, serving variously as a local councillor, including chairman of Hornchurch UDC, a county councillor, a JP, as well as participating in voluntary organisations such as the Hornchurch and Britannic Lodge Cricket Clubs, of which he was president. Among his contributions to the area was the Jubilee Youth Centre, and his name is appropriately commemorated in the Robert Beard Youth Centre on the former Hornchurch Hall Estate. He had shrewd business judgment which he put to good effect: in November 1934, for instance, along with Walter Bonnett, he bought 117 acres of Suttons Farm for £30,750, selling to Leftley Bros. in March 1937 for £38,000, a clear profit of £7,250 (almost 25 per cent). An even better profit had been realised a few years earlier. In October 1931 Beard had bought the 199-acre Elm Farm from Walter Vellacott for £35,000. Less than two years later in July 1933 this was sold for £54,700 to Richard Costain Ltd as part of their land assembled for the Elm Park Estate.

The 146-acre Grey Towers Estate was sold in January 1929 by Mrs Elizabeth Parkes for £20,000 to Allen Ansell. He immediately sold at a profit of £2,500 to Grey Towers Estates, a company specifically formed by Frederick and Ernest Legg to develop this estate. The Leggs themselves built on the part of the estate nearest to Grey Towers

Houses on Burnway, off North Street, early 1930s.

The former lodges of Grey Towers flank the recently built Grey Towers Avenue, *c.* 1935.

mansion itself, while blocks of land were sold off to other developers, with land west of the brook running through the estate being sold to Thomas A. Clark, who developed Lyndhurst, Grosvenor and Elmhurst Drives. The main development was the lengthy Osborne Road, running parallel to the south of the Romford-Emerson Park rail line, to join up with the older western end of the road. Many developers were at work there from 1929 onwards, with one of the main ones being C.A. Piper.

In its review of 1932, the *Romford Times* reported that 'although the mad rush to build houses was not so marked as in the preceding years steady development has been taking part throughout the district. Where there were green fields twelve months ago there are now brand new houses, with brand new tenants. Plans have also been afoot to start building in the vicinity of Wingletye-lane and in the neighbourhood of the railway station building operations have been given an added impetus by the opening of the electrified railway.'

The late 1930s marked the final stage in the development of central Hornchurch. In July 1936 the seventeenth-century Suttons Gate, one of the last remaining Hornchurch landmarks, was demolished. In March 1938 the 150-year-old barn in Suttons Lane, formerly part of Suttons Gate, was demolished to make way for shops, while a few months later Suttons Lodge, home of Robert Beard, met the same fate.

In the two decades after the end of the Second World War and before the creation of the London Borough of Havering some 11,000 private sector homes were completed in the Hornchurch UDC area. After a flurry of activity in 1946 and 1947, when over 600 homes were built, there was little activity until 1952 when the pace of development rose sharply, almost doubling each year from 185 in 1951, to 385 in 1952, 631 in 1953 and 1371 in 1954. The peak year was 1955 when 1,857 homes were built, after which numbers progressively declined over the next decade.

Shops at the junction of Lyndhurst Drive and Osborne Road, on the former Grey Towers Estate.

Public sector housing was not on the same scale but nevertheless the Hornchurch UDC built 3,000 homes on over twenty separate estates in the same twenty-year period. The main developments in Hornchurch were: Elm Park – 1,146; Hacton Farm – 548; Dovers Farm – 418; Maylands Green – 174; Park Lane/Brentwood Road – 159; Abbs Cross Lane – 133; Fyfield Road – 87; Princes Park – 50; Elmhurst Drive – 47; Ravenscourt Grove – 46; and Osborne Road – 24. By 1964 the council had started its first high-rise flatted estate, the 570-units Mardyke Estate, comprising 267 units in six 12-storey blocks, as well as smaller blocks.

8. SUTTONS FARM AIRFIELD

By early 1915 during the First World War Hornchurch had grown accustomed to the military presence in the village with the Sportsman's Battalion billeted at Grey Towers camp. To the south of Hornchurch Station, Thomas Crawford farmed his 384-acre Suttons Farm, formerly the ancient manor of Suttons, just as he had since 1888.

But from the spring of 1915 the residents of Hornchurch were reminded of the threat of the enemy at close hand as the sight and sound of German airships passing overhead on their way to attack London became a regular occurrence. The War Office decided to counter this threat by setting up a string of defences around the capital and 90 acres of Suttons Farm were requisitioned to form Temporary Landing Ground II of the Royal Flying Corps. This was a rather primitive facility equipped with a pair of BE2c observation planes, temporary canvas RE5 hangars, fuel and equipment. The L-shaped grass landing strip was just 300 yards long, within an airfield 500 yards square. Two rows of petrol cans, with their lids removed and crammed with petrol-soaked rags, provided the illumination for night-time take-offs and landings.

As the German aerial threat continued the facilities at Suttons Farm were improved. More permanent wooden sheds replaced the canvas hangars, and workshop facilities and living quarters were added, the latter converted from wooden aircraft crates. From April 1916 the airfield became home to 39 (Home Defence) Sqn, by now equipped with six BE2cs, modified for use as night-fighters, each with a single Lewis machine-gun mounted on the centre section of the upper wing. Without the benefit of wireless communications, oxygen equipment, cockpit heating – or even the escape route of a parachute – night-fighter pilots were expected to locate and destroy the high-flying enemy airships. Despite their lack of success in their many attempts to intercept and destroy the raiders throughout the summer of 1916, the RFC pilots gained valuable experience and a greater co-ordination of aircraft movements and anti-aircraft ground defences was developed.

The single incident that gained national recognition for the names of Suttons Farm and Hornchurch came on the night of 2/3 September 1916. Up to then the airship raids

A night-fighter Camel comes in to land at Suttons Farm, c. 1916. The four wooden hangars and the tented staff accommodation can be seen. (Hornchurch Historical Society)

Artist's impression of attack on airship *SL21* prior to its destruction over Cuffley, 2/3 September 1916.

on London and surrounding areas had continued without any significant interruption and the RFC pilots seemed powerless to halt these regular enemy incursions. It was on this night that a German airship was shot down in flames for the first time, and more significantly the pilot concerned – Lt William Leefe Robinson – was well known to many Hornchurch villagers as he had been based at Suttons Farm for the past seven months.

Sixteen German airships had taken part in the raid that night on what was to prove the single greatest air-raid of the war. As on previous occasions, the village of Hornchurch was alive with many spectators watching the gun-flashes and searchlights as the intruders moved towards London. Suddenly at around 2 a.m. the sky was brilliantly lit and an airship was seen falling to earth in flames. Three hours earlier, at just after 11 p.m. on a beautifully clear night with little cloud, Robinson and his colleague Lt Frederick Sowrey had taken off in their BE2cs on a normal night patrol in the area between Suttons Farm and Joyce Green in Kent. At 1.10 a.m. Robinson saw an airship lit up by two searchlights near Woolwich. He changed course and increased height to intercept it, but the airship entered a cloud and was lost to sight. Almost immediately Robinson sighted a red glow over London, caused by the effect of bombs dropped on Edmonton and Ponders End by the naval airship *Schutte Lanz SL21*, captained by Hauptmann Wilhelm E.L. Shramm.

Changing the previously unsuccessful tactics, Robinson began a diving approach from 12,000 feet to gain speed until he came within 800 feet below the cigar-shaped raider. After firing two complete drums of bullets along the length of the ship on his first two approaches Robinson returned to concentrate the fire from his last drum of ammunition on one small section of hull. Almost at once the target began to glow, the rear part rapidly burst into flames and the craft fell towards earth out of control. By now Robinson's BE2c had been airborne for well over two hours and was low on fuel so he had to return to Suttons Farm, landing at 2.45 a.m. His flaming victim came to earth in a field at Cuffley, Hertfordshire, with the loss of its sixteen-man crew.

After months of seemingly ineffective defence against the German air attacks the population reacted almost hyster-ically to Robinson's fiery success, showering him with adulation. Almost instantly, just two days later on 5 September, he was awarded the Victoria Cross, which was invested on the new national hero by King George V at a special ceremony at Windsor Castle on 8 September. The modest lieutenant was also the recipient of countless gifts, including 'prize' contributions totalling £4,200, some of which he used to buy a Vauxhall 'Prince Henry' automobile.

William Leefe Robinson had been born in India in 1895, the youngest son of Horace Robinson, a coffee planter, and Elizabeth née Leefe. After leaving St Bees public school in Cumbria he went

Lt William Leefe Robinson VC.

on to the Royal Military College, Sandhurst, just after the outbreak of war in August 1914, and was commissioned lieutenant with the Worcester Regiment on 16 December 1914, transferring to the Royal Flying Corps in February 1915. Following his exploits of the night of 2/3 September 1916 Robinson requested a less public role and was soon promoted to captain and transferred to a new unit which moved to France in March 1917. Just three weeks later on 5 April Lt Robinson was shot down in action over France, spending the remainder of the war in a series of prison camps, from which he attempted to escape several times. During his captivity he was often kept in solitary confinement and harshly treated, as a result of which his health suffered. By the Armistice of November 1918 he was already a sick man, and after being repatriated to England he died at Stanmore, Middlesex, on 31 December 1918 from heart failure, brought on by the virulent influenza virus which was sweeping Europe at that time. He was buried with full military honours at All Saints' church, Harrow Weald, three days later, aged just twenty-three years old.

Robinson's historic plane came to an untimely end two weeks after his triumph, written off after catching fire when he crashed into a hedge on take-off. The following week, on Saturday 23 and Sunday 24 September 1916, Capt Robinson was again on duty at Hornchurch when a Zeppelin dropped six bombs in the area, one falling in the aerodrome itself, although no damage was done and only one person was slightly injured. The raiders continued on towards London, where they caused considerable damage in a raid during which many people died or were injured. Just before 1 a.m., a crimson glow lit the sky and the countryside around as Zeppelin *L.32* fell to earth near Billericay. Soon after, an aeroplane returned to Suttons Farm and it was not long before Capt Robinson's car, filled with officers from the airfield – including the hero of the night, Lt Frederick Sowrey – sped off to visit the burning wreckage. And just eight days later, on 1 October 1916, the 'hat-trick' of victories for pilots from Suttons Farm was completed when Lt Wulstan J. Tempest became the third Hornchurch flyer to down a Zeppelin, this time *L.31*, brought down at Potter's Bar. Both Sowrey and Tempest were rewarded with the DSO for their achievements.

On 15 September, as part of the celebrations of Robinson's success, he had been presented with an inscribed silver inkstand by the children at the Hornchurch Cottage Homes. Four weeks later on 16 October, after the other two successes, there was a presentation in recognition of the three airmen's exploits at the New Zealand Forces camp, Grey Towers, in the presence of a large crowd. Each of the three Hornchurch-based heroes received a suitably inscribed silver cup 'as a token of admiration and gratitude' from the people of the village, over 2,000 of whom had subscribed between 1*d* and 2*s* 6*d* for the gifts.

From early 1917 the Zeppelin threat had virtually lifted but within a few months the Germans adopted new tactics. On 13 June 1917 a fleet of Gotha bombers made a daylight bombing raid on the east end and City of London, killing 157 and wounding 432. The perpetrators of these raids on the capital were visible as they passed high over Hornchurch in broad daylight on their journey to and from London. During the late

Lt Robinson receives his cup, 16 October 1916. Lt Frederick Sowrey is on the right.

summer and early autumn of 1917 there were many heavy night raids on London too. To the people of Hornchurch these raids were nerve-racking, as they could hear the drone of the aircraft but could not see the raiders, except when located by a spotlight. As London's air defences were strengthened the Germans found these raids increasingly costly in terms of aircraft and manpower and they were abandoned after May 1918. Suttons Farm had remained in use throughout this time as a day and night-time flying ground but, with the lifting of the enemy threat, the airfield became a night-flying scout training base.

Although the airfield was steadily run down after the end of hostilities, the memories of the Hornchurch airmen's successes were still fresh when in 1920 Suttons Farm was returned to its tenant farmer Tom Crawford. But a review of the country's defence needs was soon underway and this led to teams from the Air Ministry being sent off in a search of suitable sites for airfields within a 10- to 20-mile radius of the capital. When they visited Tom Crawford's farm in November 1922 they found that it was divided into three fields growing potatoes, turnips and clover. Some airfield buildings still existed, including former WRAF accommodation now used as an outhouse for Romford Union Workhouse, but other buildings, although only five or six years old, were generally in poor condition and unlikely to be suitable for integration into a new airfield.

In June 1923 Prime Minister Stanley Baldwin announced proposals for the creation of a Home Defence Force of fifty-two RAF squadrons. Hornchurch was chosen as a suitable airfield site and in July 1923 compulsory purchase powers were agreed by the Treasury. The owners, New College, Oxford, agreed to sell 120 acres of Suttons Farm to the Air Ministry, although they asked that the airfield boundary should be at least 300

A serviceman guards the entrance to the new Hornchurch aerodrome, 1928. (RAF Hornchurch Association)

yards from Suttons Farmhouse. As a result the airfield layout had to be replanned, and over the next few years additional land adjoining the site, including parts of Algores Farm and also land to the west of South End Road, was bought to make up for these losses. Building started as early as May 1924 but with the changes to the layout and the delays in acquiring extra land it was almost four years until the new airfield opened on 1 April 1928, changing its name a few months later to RAF Hornchurch.

9. RAF HORNCHURCH

The focal point of the new RAF Hornchurch airfield switched from the proposed Suttons Farm area to that adjoining South End Road where the new entrance was sited. From the entrance the main roadway led to the 175-foot C-type gabled hangar, passing the guardroom on the left, just inside the gates, with a flagpole flying the RAF ensign. Around the whole perimeter ran a gravelled track about 6 yards wide. Off the main drive, side roads ran off to the right and left leading to mess rooms, accommodation, operational buildings and various store sheds which formed the 53-acre technical site. On the opposite side of South End Road, furthest from the flying fields, was the Officers' Mess and other living accommodation. The whole site was framed with neat flowerbeds, shrubs and lawns which reflected the highly disciplined image of an RAF airfield.

The annual routine for the airmen at the camp was soon established, including armament practices, practices for the annual Air Display at RAF Hendon and night-flying trials. To the citizens of Hornchurch, camp personnel became a common sight in the area, particularly in local pubs such as the adjacent Good Intent, the King's Head and, after 1935, at the Towers Cinema. Establishing good community relations was important to the RAF and cricket, football and other sporting teams from the airfield played fixtures with local teams. But perhaps the most visible evidence of this was the annual Empire Air Day held from 1935 onwards, when the airfield was opened for the general public to enjoy a programme of aerial displays and fly-pasts. And because the airfield was located alongside South End Road thousands more spectators watched for free. After the opening of Elm Park Station in May 1935 people from near and far could more easily visit the area, becoming increasingly attracted to weekend strolls by the airfield boundary along South End Road which offered an open view across the operational area.

By 1930 there were more than 400 airmen at Hornchurch and in 1936 the site was further expanded when additional buildings, including a third hangar and improved watch office, were completed. Later that year a new sector operations room was

View of RAF Hornchurch from South End Road, 1928. (RAF Hornchurch Association)

inaugurated, raising the status of Hornchurch to one of seven sector airfields in 11 Group, Fighter Command. In August 1936 the erection of a 150-foot chimney on what is now St George's Hospital, just 800 yards from the airfield, meant that night-flying had to be banned for six months until the chimney could be adequately lit.

As the Second World War approached the range of facilities in use for Home Defence was expanded. Radio Direction Finding (RDF) – known from 1943 onwards as radar (radio direction and ranging) – allowed a new system of defence and aircraft control to be developed while in 1939 trials were run on a new feature – a broadcasting system manufactured by Tannoy – which allowed the controller's instructions to be relayed to units across the whole airfield. After this successful experiment, this method became standard practice and the new loudspeaker system was universally known as 'Tannoy', after its manufacturers. Throughout the 1930s Hornchurch was RAF Fighter Command's 'shop window', and the latest fighters, from Bristol Bulldogs to Gloster Gladiators, were based there. Hornchurch was often used to display the best of what the RAF had to offer to distinguished visitors from home and abroad, increasingly those who were potential allies in the inevitable conflict.

Without a doubt the RAF's most famous fighter plane of the Second World War was the Supermarine Spitfire, designed by R.J. Mitchell and derived from a seaplane which had won the Schneider Trophy in 1931, with the addition of a Rolls-Royce PV12 'Merlin' engine. Its top speed of almost 360 mph and its armaments of eight 0.303 machine-guns made it a formidable fighting machine. On 14 February 1939 the Hornchurch base received its first Spitfire to re-equip No. 74 Sqn, and over the next eight weeks all three squadrons changed from Gloster Gladiators with few problems.

The arrival of the Spitfires boosted attendance at Empire Day Air Display in May 1939 and almost 60,000 people attended – a record 45,000 paying customers and probably another 15,000 free – all anxious to catch a glimpse of the revolutionary new aircraft.

Hornchurch was to become the most renowned of the Spitfire stations in Fighter Command. When war began Hornchurch, a sector station in No. 11 Group of Fighter Command, covered the vital south-eastern approaches to London, with satellite airfields at Rochford in Essex and Manston in Kent serving as forward fields. The Hornchurch airfield held three of No. 11 Group's six Spitfire squadrons. It was the only RAF station then to be equipped exclusively with three squadrons of Spitfires, with some 50 of the 300 on the strength of Fighter Command. Each squadron was nominally equipped with twenty pilots and sixteen aircraft, as well as the necessary groundcrew. Like other RAF stations Hornchurch had no hard-surfaced runways but a large grassy field which provided three 'runs': the north–south aligned No. 1 Flightway of 1,200 yards; and Nos 2 and 3 Flightways, each just short of half a mile, running roughly west to east. The latter two runways crossed South End Road, which was from 1941 closed to traffic near to the Good Intent.

Spitfires from 65 Sqn RAF Hornchurch, 1939. (RAF Hornchurch Association)

During the early days of the war the RAF – and the country – believed a German attack was imminent. All squadrons were kept on a state of 'readiness', ready to take off within five minutes. In this tense state it was perhaps inevitable that tragic mistakes would occur. One such incident was the so-called 'Battle of Barking Creek' on 6 September 1939 when anti-aircraft batteries opened fire on Hurricane fighters from North Weald, mistakenly identified as German Me109s. In the confusion, three Spitfires from 'A' Flight at Hornchurch dived to attack, shooting down two Hurricanes and killing one pilot, Plt Off Hulton-Harrap, who became the first Fighter Command pilot of the war to be killed. The pilots concerned from No. 74 Sqn at Hornchurch were acquitted of any blame at a court martial and returned to their squadron. The station had to wait two months for its first true success when a Dornier Do17 was shot down into the sea about 15 miles off Southend.

The severe winter of 1939/40, possibly the harshest in Essex for sixty years, greatly restricted operations but this state of affairs changed in May 1940 after the German advance across Holland and Belgium. The first offensive patrol from Hornchurch was on 17 May 1940 when twenty-four Spitfires from Nos 74 and 54 Sqns were in action over Ostend. The next day No. 65 Sqn gave Hornchurch its first offensive 'victory' when a Junkers Ju88 was shot down off Flushing. From late May 1940 Hornchurch

Pilots from 54 Sqn scramble, *c.* 1940. (RAF Hornchurch Association)

squadrons were in constant action in support of the nineteen-day operation to evacuate the British Expeditionary Force from Dunkirk, claiming 83 enemy aircraft destroyed but at the cost of 27 pilots. The most spectacular action was probably that which took place on 23 May when Flt Lt James 'Prof' Leathart flew an unarmed two-seater Miles Master, escorted by two Spitfires piloted by Alan Deere and Johnny Allen, in a daring attempt to rescue Sqn Ldr Francis White of No. 74 Sqn, who had been forced to land at Calais-Marck airfield, which was still in Allied hands. Heavily outnumbered and under attack from six Me109s, the two Spitfires incredibly shot down three Messerschmitts and damaged the other three, enabling Prof Leathart to escape successfully with his relieved passenger.

Deere was also involved in another interesting incident on 28 May. Shot down and forced to crash land on the Belgian coast, he made his way, by a variety of routes, to Dunkirk, where he joined thousands awaiting evacuation. He managed to be taken off on a Royal Navy destroyer which, although under attack from enemy aircraft, made it safely to Dover. The weary pilot fell asleep on the London-bound train and was awakened rudely by the guard who almost made him get off because he had no ticket, until a brigadier intervened. From Charing Cross Deere took the District Line Tube to Elm Park, arriving back at the Officers' Mess just nineteen hours after he had left it!

In June 1940 Flt Lt A.G. ('Sailor') Malan from No. 74 Sqn became the first single-seat fighter pilot of the war to down a bomber at night, destroying a Heinkel over Chelmsford, and for good measure, that same night, he brought down a Ju88 near Foulness. Arguably the finest RAF fighter pilot of the war, Malan, a South African who had joined 74 Sqn in 1936, took over as squadron leader later in 1940, aged 29, when 35-year-old Francis White was deemed too old to lead a fighter squadron. Malan notched up thirty-four victories (including shared successes) by July 1941. After a long and distinguished RAF career, in which he reached the rank of group captain and earned the DSO, DFC and two bars, he died in 1962 at the age of fifty-two.

On 27 June 1940 Hornchurch played host to Sir Hugh Dowding, Air Chief Marshal, and King George VI, who in a special investiture decorated five of Hornchurch's principal pilots. Sqn Ldr Leathart received the DSO, while DFCs were presented to Plt Off Johnny Allen and Flt Lts Al Deere, 'Sailor' Malan and Stanford Tuck.

In June 1940 on the verge of the Battle of Britain the personnel strength of the station, excluding the squadrons, was some 650 airmen and NCOs, 34 officers and 281 airwomen and 6 WAAF officers. Hornchurch squadrons were in the thick of the fighting from the first week of July, prior to the officially recognised start of the Battle of Britain on 10 July. Hornchurch was to play a crucial role in the Battle with four locally based squadrons – Nos 41, 54, 65 and 74 Sqns – bearing the brunt of the action during the first month of the Battle.

RAF pilots characteristically gained nicknames and, in addition to 'Sailor' Malan and 'Prof' Leathart, Hornchurch also had, at some time, 'Wonkey' Way, 'Treacle' Treacy, 'Broody' Benson, 'Butch' Baker, 'Ras' Berry, 'Pip' Cardell, and Eric 'Sawn-off' Lock,

King George VI presents Flt Lt Deere (54 Sqn) with his DFC, 27 June 1940. (RAF Hornchurch Association)

among others. One RAF character – this one fictitious – who emerged around this time was 'Pilot Officer Percy Prune' created at Hornchurch by Bill Hooper. The exploits of this egg-headed, button-nosed Spitfire pilot became known to every pilot in Fighter Command after his inclusion in Leathart's *Notes for Fighter Pilots* and a book called *Forget-me-nots for Fighters*.

In July 1940 Hornchurch was dealt a bitter blow through the loss on consecutive days of two seasoned pre-war veterans, Basil 'Wonkey' Way and Johnny Allen. The tall, thin Way, still only twenty-two years old but a natural leader and effective flight commander, was downed by a Me109 off Dover when on convoy patrol on 25 July. The previous day Allen, two years older with eight victories to his credit, was shot down off Margate, fatally crashing near Cliftonville. His dog, a well-known character who would sit on the lawn of the Officers' Mess awaiting his return, kept a lonely vigil for his master until darkness fell.

From 24 August onwards to the end of 1940 the Luftwaffe made fourteen attacks on Hornchurch, destroying several aircraft on the ground, damaging hangars and cratering the airfield landing area, although never badly enough to put the station out of action. The most severe attacks were perhaps those that occurred on 31 August when six Spitfires were destroyed with another five damaged, with damage to hangars, the landing

Pilots of 41 Sqn at Hornchurch with their scoreboard.
(RAF Hornchurch Association)

field, and to the domestic quarters. Hornchurch fought back well as No. 603 Sqn, which had only arrived at Hornchurch a few days before, claimed fourteen enemy aircraft for the loss of two aircraft and one pilot. The squadron's most celebrated pilot was Plt Off Richard Hillary, who accounted for five Me109s in four days before being shot down in flames on 3 September. He suffered horrendous burns and became one of the 'guinea pigs' whose injuries were treated by the first attempts at plastic surgery by Archie McIndoe at East Grinstead. Hillary returned to flying, only to be killed in January 1943. Hillary's book, *The Last Enemy*, published in 1942, is rightly considered to be one of the finest accounts of war in the air.

On 7 September 1940 the Luftwaffe changed tactics, stepping up daylight bombing offensives on London instead of the RAF fighter stations, their target since mid-August, and intensifying night attacks. Inevitably this meant a change of role for pilots from Hornchurch, whose efforts were now against the huge air armadas of fighters and bombers launched by the Luftwaffe. The respite from direct attacks allowed the Hornchurch airfield to restore communications, repair damage and deal with delayed-action bombs, and as a result defences were stronger than ever. When the invaders returned for a mass raid the following week they were turned back short of London. Another 'thousand aircraft' day occurred on 15 September, always referred to as 'The Longest Day' and now recognised as Battle of Britain Day. The Battle is officially considered (somewhat arbitrarily) to have ended on 31 October 1940. Although air raids on London continued, with heavy night bombing raids, including the massive incendiary attack on 29 December that caused widespread devastation, Hitler had by now abandoned his proposed invasion, in theory until the next spring but in practice for good. The threat to the freedom of the people of Britain had been averted. The pilots of Hornchurch had been in the thick of the Battle, flying continuously against massive raiding forces, playing a significant part in what proved to be one of the pivotal actions of the war.

From early 1941 the Hornchurch Spitfire squadrons acted as escorts to support the bombing offensive, initially by Blenheim Bombers but later by Bostons, Fortresses and

Liberators. The armaments of the Spitfire were improved and the addition of bombs allowed them to take part in low-level operations against targets on land or sea. By the end of 1941 Hornchurch was home to 78 officers, 1,269 airmen and 314 airwomen. In addition, the defence forces for the aerodrome which included six platoons of the Essex Regiment, a detachment of Royal Artillery, some Home Guard, a Canadian anti-aircraft battery, an RAF ground-defence section, and some vehicles of the Royal Tank Corps.

Throughout 1941 and 1942 the personnel at Hornchurch became increasingly cosmopolitan and international, with European and Commonwealth units attached there at various times. These included No. 313 (Czech) Sqn, No. 411 (Canadian) Sqn, No. 340 (Free French), No. 453 (Australian) and No. 485 (New Zealand) Sqns, alongside a variety of British squadrons. For their supporting role fighter squadrons were operated in 'Wings', each commanded by a wing commander (flying), who led his three or four squadrons into battle. Brendan 'Paddy' Finucane DSO, DFC, 2 bars, who arrived in June 1942, was perhaps Hornchurch's most acclaimed and legendary Wing Commander. At the time of his death on 15 July 1942 he had destroyed thirty-two enemy aircraft and this proved to be the fourth highest RAF total of the whole war.

As the nature of the war and the organisation of the RAF changed, the role and status of Hornchurch varied. With the reduced threat of German air attack in the south-east the operational role of Hornchurch was scaled down. The sector operations room was closed and the station now became a forward station under North Weald's fighter control. During late 1943 and early 1944 the Spitfire squadrons were progressively removed from Hornchurch to other bases, the last leaving on 18 February 1944. The airfield, after almost five years of feverish activity, was again quiet and the station became host to a variety of different units. In November 1944 Hornchurch became a marshalling area for troops moving to and from the battle front. By VE-Day all flying units had left and in June 1945 the airfield was passed from Fighter Command to the Technical Training Command. By this time the station had destroyed 907 enemy aircraft, with 444 probable victories in addition, at a cost of 481 pilots killed.

Hornchurch's grass runways and 1920s hangars were becoming old-fashioned and were unsuitable for the jet-engined aircraft which were introduced increasingly in later years. However, the site still made an important contribution to the RAF by providing a service for the advanced training, selection, and allocation of air crews. Between 1946 and 1962 five units in residence passed through the station: the Aviation Candidates Selection Board (1946–7); Officers' Advanced Training School (1947–8); Combined (known from 1952 as the Aircrew) Selection Centre (1948–62); Personnel Selection & Interviewing School (1951–5); and Aircrew Allocation Centre (1958–9).

By 1950 the station complement was 550 officers and airmen, 12 WRAFs, and around 110 candidates at the Combined Selection Centre. By the end of 1953 the staff

Well-attended air display at RAF Hornchurch, 1950s. (RAF Hornchurch Association)

had reduced to 430, with no WRAFs, and continued to fall to 394 in July 1955, 334 by the end of 1955 and 309 twelve months later. From time to time personnel from the station were put to a range of emergency uses including the power strike of 1949, the dock strike of April 1950 and the east coast floods of February 1953. By the end of 1958 staff numbers had reduced significantly to just 13 officers and 124 airmen and RAF Hornchurch was beginning to look ominously empty.

Despite this progressive run-down the airfield's presence was still felt locally. An 'At Home' Open Day, including a fly-past, on 17 September 1949 attracted 20,000 visitors, paying admission of 1s by programme. On Coronation Day 1953 there was a march through Hornchurch town, which assembled at the airfield and included an RAF contingent. The final station air show was held in 1960.

In 1963 the Aircrew Selection Centre moved into purpose-built facilities at RAF Biggin Hill, and the last unit vacated Hornchurch on 9 April 1962 signalling the end of a proud era. A small holding party acted as caretakers for three months but on 1 July 1962 RAF Hornchurch was formally closed. Over six months later on 27 February 1963 the majority of the station was put up for sale by auction in nine lots, Lots 1 to 7 comprising the 53½-acre Technical Site, Lot 8 the Officers' Mess, and Lot 9 open land.

Most of the Technical Site was described as having planning permission for warehousing and storage, including offices, although one lot of around 9 acres was possibly intended for residential use. Lot 7 – 8.6 acres – and the larger Lot 9 – 38 acres adjacent to Suttons Lane – were open grassland for which planning permission for gravel extraction had been requested.

Part of the Technical Site was bought by the Maylands Green Estate Company and Romford Construction Company. In the late 1960s and early 1970s this area was developed for housing on both sides of the South End Road. The landing area of the airfield itself became the East London Quarry of Hoveringham Gravel Company and when all the gravel had been extracted in the 1970s the resulting large hole was converted into a rubbish infill tip. But this was an undignified end for a once proud site has gradually been reversed from 1980 onwards by the development of the landing and operational area by the London Borough of Havering as Hornchurch Country Park. From the car park, fittingly approached along first Airfield Way and then Squadron's Approach, the pathway follows the airfield's eastern perimeter track from which several airfield features, including aircraft dispersal bays, air-raid shelters, turrets, gun emplacements and pill-boxes can be seen.

Nearby, other historic connections with the RAF are preserved as roads on new estates record the names of famous airmen who flew from Hornchurch, such as Bader Way, Malan Square, Deere Avenue, Leathart Close, Tuck Road and Finucane Gardens. To the north of the airfield in the grounds of Mitchell Primary School, which opened on 6 September 1967 taking its name from the creator of the Spitfire, is a small permanent memorial. This incorporates a replica of the RAF station badge and commemorates the latter thirty-four years of the area's service history from 1928 to 1962, oddly ignoring the earlier distinguished service. The memorial was the outcome of a memorial fund raised by public subscription and a council grant following a three-year campaign launched by Ted Exall. On 5 July 1983 it was unveiled before a crowd of several hundred, including twenty former Spitfire pilots. And further afield is another memorial of a kind: the entrance gates from RAF Hornchurch have been preserved, being transferred originally to RAF Kenley in Kent and later, when that station closed, to RAF Biggin Hill.

10. LOCAL GOVERNMENT

The historic role of the church vestry as the principal local administrative body ended in 1894 with the election of the first parish council under the Local Government Act. Parish councils were popular with local people, but their powers were limited to areas such as acquiring land for public purposes, particularly allotments, and matters concerning charities, roads, and rights of way, public lighting, and fire brigade, etc.

The election of the first Hornchurch Parish Council on 17 December 1894 was hotly contested, with seventeen candidates for the thirteen places, needing a formal ballot with the three polling stations open from 8 a.m. to 8 p.m. The inaugural parish council, which held its first meeting on New Year's Eve 1894, comprised a good mix of representatives. Henry Compton, gentleman, was the first chairman, and the other council members were Charles Henry Baker, grocer and draper, Dick Bonnett, farmer of South Hornchurch, Alfred Death of Harold Wood, clerk, John Ferguson, a dealer, William Jackson, farmer of Bush Elms Farm, John Little, estate developer of Brentwood Road, Alfred Norris, licensed victualler, Walter Paxton of Little Langtons, Frederick Playle, plumber, George Rayment, wheelwright, John Stone, market gardener and Joseph Turner of Suttons Lane, engineer.

The powers of the parish council were limited. Many local powers rested with the new Romford Rural District Council, which took over responsibilities of the former Romford Rural Sanitary Authority covering a wide area around Hornchurch with responsibilities for approving new building plans, disposing of refuse, control of nuisances, and medical health. Whereas the parish council had a single salaried clerk, the rural council had a clerk, surveyor and medical officer, as well as assistants. The parish council could successfully lobby the rural council to improve local conditions. In January 1899, for instance, a parish meeting approved a proposal for a main drainage scheme for Village ward, which eventually was adopted by the rural council in 1902.

The first Council Cottages in Hornchurch erected in Abbs Cross Lane in 1918.

Another success was the pressure applied on the Romford authorities to build 'workmen's housing' in Hornchurch, which finally led the RDC to build eighteen municipal cottages in Abbs Cross Lane in 1913.

Until the council offices and small hall were built in Billet Lane in 1915, the parish council met in the old boys' schoolroom on Church Hill. Building work started in April 1915, on a site which had been presented by the late Colonel Holmes of Grey Towers, and was completed that October.

The Hornchurch Fire Brigade provided perhaps the most tangible evidence of the work of the parish council. In 1894 the new parish council took over the manual fire engine which was housed at Hornchurch Brewery and moved it to the old Drill Hall in Billet Lane. In 1898 a uniformed voluntary fire brigade was set up under the captaincy of Edgar Bratchell, the well-known local builder, who remained in charge for more than twenty-five years until 1924. In 1900 the brigade was equipped with a new 22-man manual engine from Shand Mason & Co., which from July 1907 was housed in the new fire station on Billet Lane. There was also a sub-station in north-west Hornchurch at the Durham Arms in Brentwood Road. All parts of the parish were supplied by water hydrants, except in parts of South Hornchurch which had no water mains.

Street lighting was also a function of the parish council. Until 1895 Village ward was partly lit by the voluntary efforts of some parishioners who subscribed to a Gas Lighting Fund. On 8 November 1895 the committee controlling this fund handed over all lamps and lamp posts to the parish council. The Lighting & Watching Act 1833 was then adopted for lighting Village ward (58 lamps) and North-west ward (94 lamps). But three parts of Hornchurch were still left unlit: Harold Wood; Emerson Park and Nelmes; and that part of the parish to the south of the Midland Railway line. Two polls held in the first two districts failed to gain the necessary two-thirds majority.

Some local people were resentful that the RDC controlled many issues affecting Hornchurch. Resentment was deepest in the heavily populated north-west of the parish bordering Romford, which suffered serious flooding from the River Rom at times. Efforts to get the RDC to address this had proved unsuccessful. Residents felt that the roads and paths in neighbouring Romford town, under the control of its own urban district council, were superior to those in north-west Hornchurch.

Many felt that seeking urban powers and status as an urban district council would give more local control. The first serious attempt to seek urban powers came in 1911 but, after a series of public meetings and a poll, the parish council's recommendation to apply was considerably outvoted, particularly those in Village ward who felt that Hornchurch was still 'truly rural'. In the 1920s the subject of urban power was again raised, and in 1924 the parish council voted nine to five to apply for urban powers. However, public opinion in Hornchurch was divided, with opposition led by the Ratepayers' Association, whose membership, predominantly drawn from the Emerson Park and Nelmes Estates, felt that 'the time was not ripe' for urban powers.

The coat of arms designed by W. Gurney Benham of Colchester, a noted Essex historian, and adopted by Hornchurch UDC in 1926. The motto 'A good name endureth' has its origin in the Apocryphal Book of Ecclesiasticus, Ch. 41, v.13: 'A good life hath but a few days; but a good name endureth forever.' A formal grant of these arms was only made in 1948.

After a conference of representatives of all parish councils and parochial committees in the Romford RDC area failed to reach any agreement on the applications for urban powers from Hornchurch and Dagenham, the rural council decided to oppose the application. Essex County Council arranged an inquiry, which was planned to be held at Romford Institution (now Oldchurch Hospital) at the end of May 1925.

Meanwhile, the parish council elections in April 1925 were fought not on party political lines but solely on whether candidates were for or against urban powers. The 'urbanites' gained a narrow election victory by eight votes to seven, but the 'antis' claimed a moral victory, as their candidates had polled some 300 votes more than their opponents.

At the inquiry in May 1925, held in the Guardian's Board Room at Oldchurch, the Hornchurch parish clerk, Mr W.C. Allen, presented the case for Hornchurch, based on three counts: that Hornchurch was no longer rural; that it met the definition of urban; and that the present system prohibited good local government, particularly because the rural councillors were increasingly overworked. The opponents claimed that Hornchurch was still predominantly rural, that the current rural council was efficient, and that the applicants had not proved their case. Glyn Richards, the long-standing editor of the *Romford Recorder*, recalled many years later that it was 'the brilliant advocacy and presentation of the case' by the clerk Allen that made the grant of urban powers a foregone conclusion. The inquiry chairman took only a short time to conclude that both Dagenham and Hornchurch should be granted urban powers.

W.C. Allen had joined Hornchurch as assistant clerk in 1910, becoming clerk in 1913 when the incumbent Harry Perkins was dismissed for making fraudulent entries, the same crime for which his predecessor, Frederick Stratford, had been dismissed and subsequently jailed. Under Allen there were no such accusations of impropriety. He became clerk to the new UDC in 1926 and to the expanded council in 1934. The council was highly efficient from the outset and remained so until the end. Glyn

Richards regarded Hornchurch UDC as William Allen's 'best memorial'. Allen retired in January 1946 and, for his prestigious services, he was awarded the OBE.

On 1 April 1926 the new Hornchurch UDC came into being, taking over the powers of the Hornchurch Parish Council and other powers transferred from the Romford RDC. Twenty-eight candidates contested the elections for thirteen vacancies, with the newly elected council consisting of six Ratepayers, four Labour and three Independents. Five committees of the urban district were appointed: Building, Housing and Town Planning; Highways; Public Health and Sanitary; General Purposes; and Finance. Committee meetings were held three evenings monthly, with the first and most important committee taking up a whole evening, while the second and third, and fourth and fifth, each shared an evening's business respectively.

With the expanded local government powers the Billet Lane Council Offices became increasingly unsuitable. In August 1928 this accommodation problem was solved through the generosity of W. Varco Williams JP and his daughter Mrs Elizabeth Parkes, who gave their house Langtons in Billet Lane to the Hornchurch Urban Council for use as offices. Mr Varco Williams had been a long-standing Hornchurch resident, but due to ill health he had relinquished his public and business engagements and had left Hornchurch to live on the Isle of Wight. He now wished to leave the parish 'a memento of the many happy days and pleasant life' he had spent there. To avoid tax liability

Langtons House, given as a gift to Hornchurch UDC in 1929.

The ornamental lake and grounds of Langtons, which under the deed of gift must be opened to the public.

Langtons and its 5½-acre ornamental landscaped grounds and lake were given to his daughter Mrs Parkes, who formally gifted it to the local council on 1 June 1929. A condition of the gift was that the house must be used for council purposes and the grounds opened to the public.

The council's new acquisition was a three-storey red-brick mansion containing some twenty-two rooms. Langtons had been rebuilt in the eighteenth century, on the site of a much older house known in the fifteenth century as Marchaunts, and some of the original rooms survive behind the south front. During the late eighteenth and early part of the nineteenth century the house had been owned by the Massu family, wealthy silk weavers based in the City of London. Mary Massu, widow of John (d. 1807), lived at Langtons until her death in 1850, when John Wagener, a German-born sugar merchant, became the owner. After the deaths of John Wagener in 1884 and his wife seven years later the ownership of Langtons passed to their son-in-law, Colonel Holmes, who sold the property to Mr Williams in 1899. Williams remodelled the house early in the twentieth century, rebuilding the south front, opening up part of the ground floor into a staircase hall, and adding a billiard-room on the west side. Langtons continued in use as council offices until 1965 after Hornchurch became part of the new Borough of Havering. For many years it has been the Borough Superintendent Registrar's Office and a popular wedding venue.

Council meetings at Hornchurch were often stormy affairs, sometimes marked by personal animosity. This is not surprising given that the council's political make-up was a fluctuating balance between Ratepayers, Labour and Independents and bearing in mind the fiercely contested battle over the bid for urban powers. Against this turbulent background in 1933 a review of local government reorganisation was held before a Ministry of Health inspector. Romford and Hornchurch UDCs both put forward competing claims for expansion, Romford seeking to take into its boundaries the adjacent parts of north-west Hornchurch and Harold Wood. The inspector decided in favour of Hornchurch. Harold Wood and north-west Hornchurch remained as part of Hornchurch UDC, which was further expanded to take in Upminster, Cranham, Rainham, Wennington, part of Great Warley and part of North Ockendon. It was small consolation to Romford that its area was extended to include Havering-atte-Bower and Noak Hill. The decision made Hornchurch one of the biggest urban districts in the country, with an area of around 20,000 acres and a population of approximately 60,000. Romford unsuccessfully sought to overturn the decision.

The expanded Hornchurch UDC came into being on 1 April 1934. The new council's representation was increased to twenty-one, with eight wards, five of them formerly part of Hornchurch. The new council soon put forward ambitious plans for a new civic centre in Billet Lane. In December 1936 the council bought for £7,500 the 5½-acre site named Fairkytes Meadow (formerly Billet Mead and Little Billet Mead), once the site of the Fairkytes iron foundry but at that time used as a cricket and hockey

A meeting of the Hornchurch UDC in session, 1950s.

ground by Hornchurch Cricket Club. The civic centre plans were put on hold and resurrected in the late 1950s. In 1960 the house known as Little Langtons, on the east side of Billet Lane, was bought as part of this project, but after Hornchurch became part of the new London Borough of Havering the plans were dropped. This site became a car park while the proposed civic centre site was later developed for the new Queen's Theatre.

By 1956 Hornchurch UDC owned 471 acres of open spaces, of which 313 acres were in the ancient parish of Hornchurch. The largest public open space was the 120-acre Harrow Lodge Park. This included Harrow Lodge Farm, which was part of the adjacent Hornchurch Cottage Homes Estate along Hornchurch Road from the Cottage Homes and bordered on the east by Abbs Cross Lane. This 42-acre holding was bought by Hornchurch UDC from London County Council for £16,250 in April 1936. Eight months later a further 35 acres were added, when Costains, the developers of Elm Park, gave the council part of Wyebridge Farm.

Harrow Lodge itself, a stuccoed late eighteenth-century house, became Hornchurch's first public library, the branch opening later in 1936. Public libraries, however, were not part of the UDC's responsibilities and this function was provided by Essex County Council. A second library came three years later with the opening of a branch in a shop at South Hornchurch. Hornchurch's main branch library transferred from Harrow Wood to Fairkytes in Billet Lane in 1953.

Harrow Lodge Park, Hornchurch.

Fairkytes, Billet Lane, in the mid-1930s. It was acquired by Hornchurch UDC in 1950.

The first record of Fairkytes dates from 1520, although the present house dates from the mid-eighteenth century. This was the home of Thomas Wedlake, whose first iron foundry was built opposite. After the deaths of Thomas and his wife Mary Wedlake in 1843 and 1846 respectively, Fairkytes was sold by their daughter and her husband in 1852 for £1,000, and subsequently was acquired by Colonel Holmes of Grey Towers. Joseph Fry, son of the well-known prison reformer Mrs Elizabeth Fry, was a tenant here during the late Victorian period. According to Perfect, Fry and his wife 'were well known in the village for their charity and benevolence. Fairkytes was, during their occupancy, the centre of activity for all kinds of parochial, religious and charitable work.' Joseph Fry died on Christmas Day 1896, aged eighty-seven.

Colonel Holmes sold Fairkytes and associated land in September 1902 for £3,625 to William Booth Bryan, chief engineer of the Metropolitan Works Board. This was bought for his daughter Winifred and her husband James Robertson. Born in Edinburgh, James Robertson had been appointed chief engineer of the London, Tilbury and Southend Railway in 1899, transferring to the similar position of sectional engineer after the merger with the Midland Railway in 1912. He represented Hornchurch on Essex County Council from 1920 onwards and held many other representative roles, including Justice of the Peace. He was attending a business meeting at Warley Hospital when he died suddenly in June 1926, aged seventy-four. The year after the death of his widow Winifred in October 1949, Fairkytes was sold to Hornchurch UDC, becoming a library in 1953. In the early 1950s Essex County Council earmarked the site of the White House (No. 32 North Street) and adjacent Wedlake's Cottages (Nos 34 to 48)

The Hornchurch Swimming Baths, Harrow Lodge Park, built in 1956.

for both a library and a fire station. The site was finally bought in May 1958 and cleared a few years later. A new fire station was built in 1963, but the library was only finally completed by the London Borough of Havering in 1967. Fairkytes and Harrow Lodge libraries were then closed.

As the council grew first to twenty-seven members in 1948 then with a rise to thirty in 1952, the political make-up changed. In the 1930s the UDC had been dominated by the Hornchurch Ratepayers' Association, whose hold on the council progressively got stronger, but after the war the balance of control swung between the Labour and Conservatives. In 1956 with an estimated population of 110,000 Hornchurch was the second largest urban district in England; by 1964 its population was estimated to be 133,000. The urban district's ambitions matched its size. After the war it had embarked on a large municipal housing scheme, built the Harrow Lodge indoor swimming pool in 1956 at a cost of £160,000, and had joined with Romford Borough Council and Thurrock Urban District Council to build the South Essex Crematorium at Corbets Tey, which opened in June 1957.

11. HORNCHURCH HIGH STREET

When I first saw our village High Street, with its ancient gabled houses, projecting stories, dormer windows, and curiously carved and moulded fronts, it was still to a large extent unspoiled by modern 'improvements', and it can be readily imagined that when that picturesque street, with its cobbled sidewalks, and North Street, Church Hill, Billet Lane, Suttons Lane and Wingletye Lane, with the beautiful old church on the hill-top, and the ancient windmill at the far end of the Dell, together with the outlying farmsteads, comprised the whole of the village (as distinct from the parish), the inhabitants were well content with their pleasant surroundings.

The above quotation was written by Charles Perfect in 1917, describing Hornchurch village as it was when he first arrived in 1902. Even in that year Perfect could describe this central area as the 'old village' which could 'generally be described as of the 17th century, and many of the shops and small houses are of that period'. But over the next few decades this changed completely and most of old Hornchurch has now disappeared. In 1925 in Hornchurch parish there were thought to be twenty-five houses dating from before 1714, but within a few years redevelopment was underway and by 1953 nine of them had gone. At that time there were still fifty houses that had been built before 1800

Hornchurch High Street, looking east from the junction with North Street towards the White Hart, *c.* 1917.

Hornchurch High Street in transition, mid-1930s. The White Hart has been rebuilt and the junction with Station Lane remodelled.

in Hornchurch but just sixteen of these survived by 1976. In central Hornchurch only ten pre-eighteenth-century houses survived in 1976, compared to the thirty-two recorded in 1953.

The destruction of Hornchurch's ancient High Street took place piecemeal over a thirty-year period but when complete almost all signs of the past had disappeared, to be replaced by a mish-mash of modern shops. Early redevelopment was at the White Hart end. In December 1932 the *Romford Times* reported that in the past year the High Street had 'altered beyond recognition. Fine new shops give a hint that Hornchurch may shortly throw out its challenge as a shopping centre.' Plans to widen the High Street to 50 feet in width were approved in 1935 but by July 1936 the *Hornchurch and Upminster News* was campaigning against the council's reluctance to make a priority of 'the widening of this danger spot', claiming that 'the majority of residents . . . desire that the matter should be pushed through with all speed'. The paper urged that 'the High-street [be] made into a thoroughfare worthy of the community . . . merely to knock off a few feet here and there to open up the bottle neck simply will not do'. Work was scheduled for late in 1937, but little happened that year or early in 1938, although many buildings were demolished. With the intervening war years, Hornchurch's ancient High Street survived into the 1950s before demolition and redevelopment was substantially completed by 1960.

The High Street itself stretched from Abbs Cross Lane to St Andrew's church, with the portion past the White Hart known as Church Street or Church Hill until well into the twentieth century. On the north side there were no buildings from the entrance to Grey Towers (now Grey Towers Avenue) to Billet Lane, as that area formed the boundary of the Grey Towers Estate. Shops were only built there after that estate was sold in January 1929.

Before this redevelopment the tailor's shop of Albert Collin, at the eastern side of Billet Lane, was the first building on the north side. Adjacent to Collin's were Pennant's Almshouses, originally built under the will of Pierce Pennant, who died in 1590. A stone on the front of the building was inscribed with the date 1597. In 1720 a parish workhouse was built there which remained in use as a workhouse until Hornchurch was grouped with other local parishes in 1835 to form the Romford Poor Law Union. A new Union workhouse to serve the wider area was built at Oldchurch and the old Hornchurch workhouse was restored by Thomas Mashiter in 1837 and reused as an almshouse. In 1917 it comprised eight tenements, occupied by five widows and three married couples.

Next on the north side, at 101 High Street, the distinctively shaped double round-topped buildings of Page Calnan Co., builders' merchants, were located from the early years of the century until the 1970s. This site had previously been Wedlake's Union Iron Foundry. Between here and the Bull Inn were houses and, set back from the road past the Bull, was the Territorial Army Drill Hall. Built and presented by Henry Holmes of

Pennant's Almshouses and the adjacent tailor's shop of Albert Collin, 1930s.

A gaily decorated carnival passes down Hornchurch High Street, August 1910.

Grey Towers, it opened in 1892 as the home of the Hornchurch Company (No. 9) of the Essex Artillery Volunteers. After the Volunteers were superseded by the Territorial Force in 1908, the local company became the Hornchurch Company of the 4th Essex Battalion. At the outbreak of war in August 1914 this company was called up for home service, and almost all the men volunteered for foreign service, serving in Gallipoli, France and other theatres of war. As the parish had no village hall, the Drill Hall became the venue for most public meetings as well as balls, concerts and other functions.

In front of the Drill Hall stood the village pump. By the 1890s this had fallen into disuse through lack of a handle. After a lengthy debate the new parish council approached Emmanuel College, Cambridge, who owned the piece of land on which the pump stood, and the college erected a new pump. The parish council thought that they might be able to use the water from the pump to water the parish roads but the supply was hopelessly inadequate for this purpose. Soon afterwards it was discovered that the water from the pump was unfit to drink and the pump was henceforth fenced in.

The next houses (Nos 113 to 121, a terrace of five) were also owned by Emmanuel College. No. 113 housed Frost Brothers (see pp. 23–4), wheelwrights and coachbuilders, superseded by Easter Brothers, motor engineers, in the 1930s when Frosts concentrated their business at their North Street premises. At No. 121 throughout the 1920s and '30s was Robert Beard's bakers, formally described as 'R.W. Beard (Essex) Ltd', although Beard himself was familiarly known as 'Bobby'. Between

Beard's and the old Britannia Inn were four more cottages, one of which, between the wars, housed Ernie Chapman's hairdressers. Next to the Britannia was Harry Adams' butchers, the man himself recalled by Ted Ballard as 'a large jovial man with the typical blue striped butcher's apron and straw boater . . . [who] used to stand looking over the stable type bottom half of the door'. In the 1920s part of the Britannia itself was used as Henry Goodwin's refreshment rooms.

The south side of the High Street from the junction with Abbs Cross Lane to close to the Cricketers' Inn remained undeveloped until 1895. On the corner of the High Street and Abbs Cross Lane stood Red House, home to the Bratchell family from 1908 and throughout the early decades of the twentieth century. At the rear was the Bratchell's builders' yard, which during the Victorian period had been the flourishing pottery and brick and tile works of Charles Cove, described in 1851 as a 'Master brickmaker employing 18 men'. In Hornchurch church are two bell ringers' beer pitchers, dated 1731 and 1815. The later pitcher was certainly made at Cove's pottery and presented by him. It seems likely that the earlier pitcher was made there also, as the pottery is thought to have been established in the early 1700s. The pitchers had for many years been kept at Hornchurch Hall and were used for supplying refreshments to tenants when they came to pay tithes there. Later they were kept at the King's Head, from where Henry and Benjamin Holmes, when owners of the brewery, seized them in distraint of unpaid rent, placing them at Grey Towers. After the death of Colonel and Mrs Holmes they were presented to Hornchurch church.

New houses built at the western end of the High Street between 1895 and 1906 (Nos 4 to 60) comprised a mix of semi-detached and terraced cottages and villas. Nos 4 to 24 had small gardens, as did Nos 46 to 56, while the houses between were set back. Among those living here were members of the Dockrill family, carpenters and undertakers, established in Hornchurch in the carpentry trade since 1814. They later combined with Horace Fry and in 1937 J.H. Dockrill and H.G. Fry were listed in the trade directory as funeral furnishers, carpenters and monumental masons. At No. 62 in the 1920s and '30s were the well-established firm of A.G. and H. Sibthorpe, builders (later Sibthorpe and Green). In 1913 George Sibthorpe was the owner of Nos 46 to 60 and 70 to 74 High Street.

Beyond the Cricketers' Inn (No. 64) were a pair of shops, in various uses, and joined to these were the Old Cottages. These very old lath and plaster cottages opened straight off the street, some overhanging on the upper storey. The grocers of Arthur Wakeham, at No. 84 around the time of the First World War, marked the start of the shops, while through the 1920s and '30s Sydney Murphy's grocers shop occupied the premises. The adjacent shop housed Charles Evans' Brooklands farm dairy, which superseded Moss's dairy. Behind Evans' shop was a field where the cows grazed and, so the story goes, it was often possible to buy a jug of fresh milk, still warm from the cow!

At No. 88 from before the First World War well into the 1930s was George Blake's blacksmiths. Eastwards from here shops had a variety of uses over the years. Best

The Brooklands farm dairy and Arthur Wakeham's grocers, *c.* 1915. The old cottages are to the right.

recalled perhaps is George Franklyn's butchers at No. 116 from the early years of the century until the late 1920s or early '30s when A.W. Sibley continued in this trade (roughly where the Woolworth store is now situated). Set back from the road beyond Franklyn's were Appleton's Almshouses, three small brick-built houses funded by a charity established under the will of Henry Appleton in 1587. Originally offered for sale in 1939 the almshouses were eventually demolished in 1967.

Further east, roughly opposite the Britannia and the junction with North Street, was one of the village's well-known landmarks, the Old Archway. Two rooms were built over the flat timber-lined gateway and the whole premises, probably dating to the sixteenth century, were already in poor condition by the early years of the century. The passageway led through to a yard and to an old barn, burnt down in July 1934.

On the north side, at the lower end and on the east side of North Street, there were also a number of tradesmen, including Henry Brewer, greengrocer and Mr Ferguson, the butcher, whose shop was entered through an iron-studded wooden door of ancient origins. As late as 1870 a Mr Fry was carrying out a fellmonger's business on these premises. In Ferguson's front garden was situated the old cage, where in former days vagrants and other miscreants were locked up to cool off. This gave the name of Cage Row to the cottages adjacent to the Britannia. On the opposite side, towards the High Street, was the Green Lantern Restaurant, which had formerly been the fishmonger's shop of George Dawson (commonly known as 'Kippers' Dawson, for obvious reasons).

Continuing into the High Street on the north side was the newsagents and hairdresser's shop of Drake, superseded from around the time of the First World War

The cottages known as Cage Row at the lower end of North Street.

by Albert Smith's newsagent and lending library. Next door was Fred Franklyn's shoemakers, whose awning recorded that the business had been established in 1819, and then at No. 141 Edith Comber's old-fashioned dressmaker, haberdashery and draper's shop, which expanded to take over the adjacent shop. In the early years of the century, beyond the terrace of houses and small shops, was the Hornchurch Cigar Stores, with the village post office adjoining. By around 1910 this building was replaced by the high-gabled parade of three shops, which still survives as one of the older parts of the High Street. The first of these, at No. 155, was Thomas Nightingale's dairy, which in the 1930s became the United Dairies, and until a few years ago Waide Pollards, linen draper. At No. 157 was the tobacconists of Harry and later Frank Luff, whose many fine photographs have left a lasting record of old Hornchurch (this is now Pinney's solicitors), while the third premises in this parade, now Lloyds Bank, started life as the London, County and Westminster Bank.

Beyond the alleyway, which nowadays leads through to the Fentiman Way car park, was a pair of old premises, the first occupied by Bert Weever's grocer's shop around the time of the First World War, and later Fred Machin's jewellers and watchmakers, and the other Robert (later Charles) Living's estate agents and surveyors. Further down, closer to the White Hart was Fentiman's flower shop and nurseryman's business, which protruded out onto the pavement beyond the other shops. An army lorry crashed into the corner one night towards the end of the war in about 1945.

By the North Street junction, back on the south side, the road curves round. Here was Henry Gott's saddle and harness-makers business, and beyond that Charles Baker's

Soldiers and civilians waiting for the parade outside Albert Smith's newsagents, *c.* 1919.

grocers, whose square-topped premises appear prominently in early photographs taken from the corner of North Street, outside the Britannia. Charlie Baker, as he was known, played an active part in local affairs, being elected to the first parish council, and remaining a member for over twenty years. His shop in Hornchurch village became Green's Stores in the early 1920s while his other shop on Upminster Hill was later sold to Harold Moore. Between here and the White Hart shops included in the 1920s and 1930s John Read's estate agents and surveyors, Alfred Search's greengrocers, Pearce's ironmongers (originally a smithy) and John Kingdon's greengrocers.

One of the best remembered businesses is perhaps Aley's bakery at No. 162. Fred Aley came to Hornchurch in 1906, buying the baker's business from Robert Beard. He was helped by his four sons and one daughter, and after his death in 1941 the business carried on as a family affair until the shop was demolished in 1955. The site was later developed as a supermarket, later Fine Fares, and now Peacocks and Milletts clothing shop, although the road frontage was taken back to bring much needed width to a restricted part of the main road. Next to Aley's, on the corner facing the White Hart, was the Chain House, so named because of the low chain fence separating the front of the house from the pavement. Once the home of the village nurse, this was demolished in 1928 when the road-widening plans and the remodelling of this corner first started to take effect.

Originally, the main junction between Station Road – as the village end of Station Lane was styled – and the High Street was past the White Hart. On the village side there was only a passageway called White Hart Alleyway. Beyond this junction, the north side of the High Street, around the King's Head, was known as Church Hill or Church Street. These properties were mainly houses linked to the brewery opposite, and the King's Head and attached premises are the last remaining parts of old Hornchurch. One of these housed a flamboyant character recalled by many older Hornchurch residents, George Hurrell, the village window-cleaner. He openly wore make-up, including lip-stick, but is also remembered for his entertainments: he was an accomplished pianist and dancer, performing as specialities the 'Sand Dance' and 'Dying Swan'.

A little further east at No. 203 was John Cockwell's laundry, later the Romford Steam Laundry, in a property known as Alfred Cottage. Between here and the lengthy stretch running up to the junction with Wingletye Lane were just three properties. Treath, where the British Legion now stands, was a large well-built red-brick house with some eight bedrooms, five on the first floor and three attic rooms. It was used as a doctor's surgery occupied by the partnership of Drs Bletsoe, Robinson and Nichols. Dr John Bletsoe had his main surgery in Upminster and concentrated on that part of the large practice; Dr Harold Robinson covered Emerson Park mainly; while Dr Henry Wilfred Lee Nichols served the Hornchurch village catchment. Treath later became Dr McAleer's surgery. Almost opposite was Dr Thomas Lambe's surgery, at the Lodge, for many years the home of Thomas Mashiter JP. Lodge Court was developed here in the

High Street, *c.* 1917. Drake's hairdresser and newsagent will soon give way to Albert Smith while Charlie Baker's grocers on the right will be replaced by Green's Stores.

Early 1950s. The Little Flower Shop on the right projected onto the pavement. In the distance Burton's tailors can be seen on the former Britannia site on the corner of North Street and High Street.

late 1930s, taking its name from the house. Dr Lambe was a well-remembered figure, particularly for his De-Dion Burton car.

Back on the north side, beyond Treath, opposite St Andrew's church where the Robert Beard Youth Centre now stands, was Hornchurch Hall. Next was the Chaplaincy, home of the vicar and known locally as the Vicarage. When this building was first offered for development in the 1960s, it was thought by local historians and the Historic Building Division of the Greater London Council to date from the eighteenth or nineteenth century and to be of no great architectural merit. By the late 1960s vandalism had caused considerable damage, and further extensive damage was caused by a fire. This revealed a much earlier timber-framed construction, which was dated to around 1400, and further, thorough investigations and recording then took place. Efforts to preserve the badly damaged building proved fruitless and in the mid-1970s it was finally demolished to make way for the new flats in Chaplaincy Gardens, partly screened from the main road behind the old brick wall and ancient trees.

12. Pubs and Inns

In 1762 the parish of Hornchurch, including Harold Wood, had eight inns, of which four were in the village. By 1848 these numbers had both grown by one, to nine and five respectively. The presence of the Old Hornchurch Brewery ensured that several local hostelries could rely on their village brewery for supplies. In 1883 for instance, the King's Head, opposite the brewery, the Bridge House at Upminster Bridge, the Cherry Tree at South Hornchurch, and the Crown at Haveringwell were all freehold properties owned by the Hornchurch Brewery. Added to this were the leasehold property of the Old Oak at the junction of Brentwood Road and Hornchurch Road in north-west Hornchurch, while in later years the now-closed Greyhound in Hornchurch High Street, the Canteen in South Hornchurch (later renamed the Albion), and the Good Intent beerhouse in South End Road were also added to the brewery's tied houses.

Of the inns which existed in 1762 only the King's Head, now No. 189 High Street, still survives in its original buildings. These late seventeenth-century timber-framed buildings, dating from 1680, were originally a coaching inn with a rear wing. For many years they were threatened with demolition under plans to 'improve' the town centre but they are now, along with the adjoining buildings at Nos 191 and 193 High Street, Grade II listed. Following a major fire in 1966 the exterior was restored to its previous appearance but much of the interior was altered. The pub was closely associated with the brewery opposite and the bottling plant next door. Deliveries only required barrels

Cattle passing down Church Hill and the brewery, towards the Kings Head, 1917. Hornchurch Lodge is on the left.

to be rolled the short distance across Church Hill. At the turn of the century the landlord was Tom Mayne who, as a national reservist, was called up to active service in September 1914 immediately war broke out, joining the 11th Hussars. Sadly he was killed in action in France in March 1916, aged forty-five, when attached to the Royal Engineers Signals. His section officer wrote that 'I could have better spared half my section than Tom Mayne. He was always bright, willing and even tempered.' Tom's widow Amelia took over as landlord, remaining in charge until the late 1930s.

A short walk from the King's Head was the White Hart. The original inn, dating from the fourteenth or fifteenth century, burned down in November 1872. According to Perfect this 'quaint hostelry' was 'said to be the most picturesque building in the village', with gables, an overhanging front and a large sundial on its main chimney stack. It was 'known to contain some architectural remains of an ecclesiastical character' which led to speculation that they came from the original Hornchurch Priory, which may have stood on the inn site. The replacement building was a functional Victorian brick-built hotel, supplied by Ind, Coope and Co. of Romford. To the rear was the White Hart's 'beer garden', which Ted Ballard recalled had a lawn surrounded by trees and shrubs and a ring of fairy lights, which made it 'a really quaint old style favourite evening family meeting place'.

When the junction of Station Road and the High Street was redesigned in 1935 the Victorian building was replaced by the current building and the gardens gave way to the road widening scheme. In recent decades, in light with modern fashions, the historic White Hart name has been replaced, firstly by the name Madison Exchange, and in the last few years being titled the Newt and Cucumber.

Junction of Station Lane and High Street, late 1950s, with the White Hart on the right.

The Bull Inn, *c*. 1917, during the time that George Heath was landlord.

The Bull (recently renamed the Fatling & Firkin), although now heavily restored dates back to the seventeenth century. Perfect describes how eighteenth- and nineteenth-century cricket matches at Hornchurch, usually played on the Langtons Estate (later part of Grey Towers), were a major occasion and cricket elevens were entertained alternatively at the Bull Inn and the White Hart. Matches were often played for high stakes and Perfect recounts a story of a cricket match in 1825 between eleven gentlemen of Hornchurch and a similar team from Fobbing. It was won by Hornchurch after which the teams 'retired' to the Bull where 'after partaking of a most excellent dinner, provided by Mr Gooch, the landlord, they were amused by some excellent songs'. A long-serving landlord at the end of the nineteenth and early twentieth centuries was George Heath. Heath was licensee for thirty-nine years until his death in January 1928, at which time he was Ind, Coope's oldest tenant. His obituary said that he had conducted his house in an 'exemplary manner' and this led to the 'high reputation' in which the Bull was held. He was 'of genial disposition' and had 'a cheery word for everyone and had hosts of friends'. For many years Heath also ran a livery stables to the rear of the pub and served as a jobmaster, hiring out carriages and carts.

The old Cricketers' Inn was demolished in late 1938 when it was described as the next of Hornchurch's ancient monuments to face the axe. It was then regarded as one of the village's oldest buildings and was 'a type of building in which tall men must gang warily for fear of cracking their heads on outstanding parts of the ceiling and on low door lintels'.

The former public house named the Crooked Billet, which stood on the spot now occupied by the house called The Billet, gave its name to Billet Lane. The original building was of some antiquity, said to be 300 years old when it was pulled down. It was a gabled house with dormer windows and a thatched roof, and was placed further back from the road than the present house. According to Perfect, writing in 1917, the Crooked Billet had closed about fifty years previously. In fact, this closure may have taken place during the 1850s, as by 1861 it seems to have been a private dwelling.

Until 1828 alehouse keepers and licensed victuallers were certified by the justices of the peace at the county quarter sessions and their licences were reviewed annually each September. However, after 1828 this control was taken away from the justices of the peace and this led to the opening of a large number of beershops. Hornchurch was no exception: the Victorian era led to a marked expansion in the number of drinking places. Some blossomed and bloomed into public houses which today are well known. Others were short-lived and are now all but forgotten. Victorian Hornchurch boasted four other beershops or alehouses which have since disappeared.

Of these former village hostelries the Britannia had the most colourful history. This alehouse, supplied by Fielder's Brewery of Brentwood, stood on the corner of North Street (where Burton's tailors has stood since it opened in 1939), and although it was closed down about 1907 it continued as an off-licence for some time. The house was one of the oldest in Hornchurch and was reputed to have once been a rest house for monks. At its eastern end in North Street there was a large chimney stack, and part of a flank wall was built entirely of Kentish Ragstone. The inside walls were all oak panelled.

The old Britannia beerhouse, a few years after its closure in 1908.

In the Britannia's cellar were two bricked-up entrances to passages, one of which was said to run to the church, while the other was thought to run to Capel Nelmes. Ted Ballard relates how when the house was being dismantled prior to its demolition the workmen broke through a section of the cellar wall butting on to North Street. A few steps down led into a small, vaulted tunnel made of crumbling bricks; the entrance itself was so small that it could only be entered backwards. After securing a 50-yard rope to the opposite side of the cellar, the workman ventured down. For safety's sake he only went 30 or 40 yards but even so the stench was unbearable.

The last occupiers of the Britannia, Mr and Mrs Aldridge, who moved out on Good Friday 1937, claimed that in the previous four years they had seen a ghost several times in the downstairs front room. Mrs Aldridge described the apparition as a 'tall figure . . . dressed as a monk, with a brown habit, girdled at the waist, a hood thrown back on the shoulders, and sandals. Sometimes he carried a book in his hand – at other times a candle . . . there was always a deathly chill in the room . . .'.

Another former beerhouse was the Foundry Arms, located close to the Cricketers' Inn opposite the Union Iron Foundry, whose workers no doubt gave these convenient premises their custom. This seems to have been opened from the 1840s to the 1870s. The Greyhound beerhouse was located in the High Street between Thomas Pearce's blacksmiths and Henry Franklyn's bootmakers and was open from the 1860s to the 1880s. The Plough beershop seems only to have been in operation during the 1840s and '50s.

Many beerhouse keepers found that there was not enough trade for them to concentrate solely on the sale of beer. In 1851 James Franklin of the Britannia was

The rebuilt Harrow Inn, Hornchurch Road, replaced an earlier thatched building pulled down in 1894.

described as a 'Grocer, pork butcher and beer seller', while at the Foundry Arms Thomas Fry was listed as 'Beer retailer and boot maker'. An unusual combination was recorded in 1861 when the proprietor of an unidentified beerhouse in the High Street was shown as a 'Beerhousekeeper and bird stuffer'.

Even outside the village centre Hornchurch was well served with public houses and beershops. To the west of the village the present Harrow Inn in Hornchurch Road stands on the site of the original inn of the same name, pulled down in 1894. According to Perfect this ancient inn, with its thatched roof and wooded front, was typical of the old public houses in the neighbourhood, which had either been replaced by more modern buildings, or had closed completely. The inn had a very large forecourt which was needed as the Harrow was a favourite stop for the horsemen with wagons laden with farm produce on their journeys up to and from the London markets. Further along Hornchurch Road, close to the boundary with Romford at the hamlet of Haveringwell, is the Crown. The original premises were claimed to date from 1433, but this ancient building had been almost entirely rebuilt by 1923.

To the north of the village at the junction of Billet Lane and North Street at Butts Green is the Chequers Inn. This late Victorian building dates from 1899, replacing an old beerhouse of the same name, which Perfect said had a 'red tiled roof and . . . style of architecture in keeping with the other ancient houses of the village'. The Drill at Squirrels Heath is another Hornchurch premises which has its origins as a beerhouse. At Ardleigh Green the Spencer's Arms recalls another of the older Hornchurch taverns which was near to the current site. The original public house had been

The Chequers Inn can be seen across the railway bridge at Emerson Park Halt.

Beyond the Bridge House Inn is Upminster Hill and the windmill.

replaced before 1851 when the 'old Spencer's Arms' was listed. The Bridge House, Upminster Bridge, is another former Victorian beerhouse just inside Hornchurch parish.

As building development sprang up public houses were often among the services provided to the new community. This trend started with the development of the estate between Brentwood Road and Hornchurch Road (now South Street) in the 1860s. The yellow-brick Old Oak, on the junction of Brentwood and Hornchurch Roads, probably dates to around Christmas 1867, when the 99-year lease on the premises began.

The Railway Hotel, at the junction of Station Road and Kenilworth Gardens, was built at a cost of £20,000 by Ind, Coope and Co. to serve the estate developed around Hornchurch Station. The half-timbered buildings, which took eighteen months to build, opened on 19 March 1934. Not surprisingly the huge Elm Park housing development included a pub. The Elm Park Hotel at the junction of Elm Park Avenue and Elm Park (Broadway) was opened in July 1938 by Mann's.

The Good Intent on South End Road was described in 1818 as 'a beerhouse near the farm called Algores'. It began in part of a cottage, one of a row of three, and with its signboard on a post outside preserved its rustic appearance into the twentieth century. It is said that John Pamment, the occupier in 1851, chose the beerhouse name because of his wish to give cheer to the neighbourhood. George Oliver was the occupier throughout the 1860s, '70s and '80s and the establishment was bought by the Old Hornchurch Brewery in 1910. It was sold to Mann and Crossman in 1925, along with other brewery properties. The former beerhouse was rebuilt by its new owners in 1927 and later became the hostelry we now know, with its long frontage suggesting the site of the three cottages. Formerly frequented by farm workers, over many years during the twentieth century the saloon and very small, dingy public bar were a regular haunt of airmen and other staff from the airfield built alongside and behind the premises. Officially, airmen were not allowed off camp but the pub, close to the main gate, was conveniently considered to be 'in bounds', so much so that Maintenance Flight made it their headquarters when off duty. However, in 1941 during the Second World War the addition of a new runway led to the closure of South End Road and with it the Good Intent, which was turned into a NAAFI for the rest of the war. Sadly, recent renovations have removed many of the photographs and memorabilia which provided a link to its past.

The first reference to the Cherry Tree 'Publick House' dates from 1773, although the present building dates to 1935. The name, and that of Cherry Tree Lane, reflect the cherry gardens that were sited here at one time, as possibly does the Orchard Farm once found nearby. Not far from the Cherry Tree is the Albion, formerly the Canteen. In 1872 the London Rifle Brigade established a firing-range along the Ingrebourne bank, the first fire-point being near the old moat of the manor house of Great Dovers. To quench the thirst of the military men who used the firing-range Edward Blewitt, farmer and builder, built a beerhouse which he appropriately named the Canteen. The range transferred to Ferry Lane in 1910, while the Canteen acquired a full licence and continued under the name, until after Mann and Crossman bought the business in 1925. It was then renamed the Albion after the company's brewery of that name in Whitechapel Road. At some time the house was enlarged, giving it a second gable in the frontage.

Cherry Tree Hotel, South Hornchurch, before it was rebuilt in 1935.

13. SPORTS AND ENTERTAINMENTS

It is now almost impossible to visualise that the Dell, the former gravel pit just beyond the churchyard and behind Mill Park Avenue that has been obliterated by a large electricity sub-station for the past few decades, was once renowned as a major sporting venue. The grassy banks of this deep hollow formed a perfect amphitheatre which could easily accommodate thousands of spectators from miles around who gathered to witness sporting occasions.

In the eighteenth century Hornchurch's Dell was the venue of one of the most famous cock-pits in the Home Counties. When contests were held there the narrow streets of the village were choked by long lines of carriages and carts carrying large crowds of spectators. Perfect records that in 1769, for instance, the third annual cock match between the 'Gentlemen of Essex' and the 'Gentlemen of London' was fought at Hornchurch with thirty-six bouts over three nights.

The most famous sporting event to take place at Hornchurch was the prize-fight between Mendoza the Jew and John Jackson, the well-known gentleman boxer, in April 1795, described by Conan Doyle in his book *Rodney Stone*. The contest was fought out on a 24-foot stage erected in the 'most advantageous hollow', around which over 3,000 spectators, including many titled people and famous pugilists, had gathered. The fight

The amphitheatre of the Dell was a perfect venue for many spectator sports.

ended in the ninth round after just 10½ hard-fought minutes when the odds-on favourite Mendoza, who was 'quite cut up', fell exhausted and gave up.

Another sport held in the Dell was an annual wrestling contest for the prize of a boar's head. The event took place every Christmas Day, and in 1826 was said to have 'been observed from time immemorial'. The boar's head was cooked at Hornchurch Hall and was carried on a pitchfork across to the Dell where up to twenty wrestlers did battle for it. Later that evening it was feasted upon by the winner and his guests at a local public house. This long-standing annual custom was discontinued after 1868 because of local concerns about the increasingly rowdy nature of the event.

Hornchurch's cricketing heritage has been well documented. Hornchurch Cricket Club was formed in 1783 and by the following year was already winning games with ease. Between 1822 and 1834 the Hornchurch club greatly distinguished itself. By 1829 the club had remained undefeated for seven years and issued a challenge to 'all Essex', which was not taken up initially. The challenge was accepted the next year and, at a match at Woodford Wells on 1 July 1830, the Hornchurch team won easily. The next year the local eleven took on the Marylebone Cricket Club, England's foremost team. After drawing at Lord's the Hornchurch eleven suffered a bad defeat in the return match at their home pitch at Langtons Park before a crowd of 3,000. The Langtons pitch, later part of the Grey Towers Estate, was over 100 years old by the time matches were last played on it in 1914. In the 1870s the Hornchurch club merged with Upminster to become Hornchurch and Upminster United Cricket Club. After a five-year period during which the village had no cricket club, a new Hornchurch club was formed in 1889, with Colonel Holmes as president and James Robertson of Fairkytes as captain. This club continued with some success until sporting activities were curtailed in 1914 as the First World War broke out. The club resumed after the war and in 1925 the club captain James Robertson made Fairkytes Meadow in Billet Lane available to the club to use as a pitch at an annual rent of £10. The new ground, which was also used for hockey and by Hornchurch's Britannic Lodge Cricket Club, opened in April 1926. This leasing arrangement continued for many years after Robertson's death in 1927.

Until 1877 Hornchurch hosted an annual village fair each Whit Monday. The High Street was lined with booths at which could be bought 'old fashioned fairings, including the famous gilded gingerbread in all its attractive and fantastic shapes and designs'. Perhaps the highlight – at least for the children of the village – was the merry-go-round which was always placed at the High Street end of Billet Lane. In the period before the First World War an annual carnival was held each August with a procession of gaily decorated floats and vehicles making its way along Church Hill and the High Street to their destination – the park of Grey Towers.

By the end of the first decade of the century the cinema had emerged as the newest invention to capture popular imagination. All over the country moving- or motion-picture houses were being opened to profit from this craze. By October 1913 the people of Hornchurch had to travel either to Grays, where the Empire Theatre had opened in

The business premises of Robert Living, valuer and estate agent, one of the owners of the Hornchurch Cinema in Station Lane.

the High Street just before Christmas 1910, or to Romford's Picture Pavilion, South Street (later named the Victory), and the Laurie Hall, which had been converted into a cinema the previous month. On 25 October 1913 three enterprising Hornchurch businessmen – Arthur E. Cooper of Elton Lodge, Robert Living, a chartered surveyor with premises in the High Street, and Bert Gower Weavers, a High Street grocer – established a new limited company, with nominal capital of £3,000 to be raised by 2,850 preference shares of £1 and 1,500 deferred shares of 2s. The company's wide-ranging aims included providing 'theatrical, operatic, musical, cinematographic and variety enterprises and entertainments of every kind and description'. The directors each had a minimum holding of £100 of shares, and received £25 remuneration.

The site chosen for the new cinema and entertainment hall on Station Road was said to be 'undoubtedly the most suitable in the district'. It was leased on a 99-year lease at a ground rent of £25 per annum, with an option to buy the freehold for £500 within five years. The completed cost of the fully equipped building was £2,000. The cinema company proposed to charge from 3d to 1s for the twice-nightly cinema performances and from 6d to 3s per stage performance with expected weekly takings of £35 and a clear weekly profit of £15.

The subscription list for shares fell well short of the desired levels and from April 1915 onwards mortgages of £2,600 were raised to buy the site with a 50-foot frontage on Station Road and the hall used as a cinema. The estimated costs proved to be too low, for by 31 December 1914 some £3,640 had been incurred on the building and equipment and the company had a bank overdraft of £567.

The task of launching the venture successfully during the war years proved difficult, and in February 1917 a receiver was appointed. In June 1919 the cinema, hall and other assets were bought by Robert Living and the company was formally dissolved on 3 October 1919. The Hornchurch Cinema seems to have met with more success in the post-war years, becoming known as the Super Cinema. However, it appears that it was closed soon after the opening of the 2,000-seat Capitol Cinema in Upminster in October 1929. After some local debate a use was finally found for the building in early 1933. With the economic depression reaching its height the old cinema was adapted by volunteers and reopened as the headquarters of the Hornchurch Social Service Association for the relief of distress.

In August 1934 work started on laying the foundations for the new cinema for Hornchurch on a vacant site at the west end of Hornchurch High Street which had been part of the Grey Towers Estate. Over the next year some 35 million bricks were used to build the imposing Towers Cinema, along much the same lines as the Mayfair Cinema at Beacontree Heath, Dagenham. The Towers, which formed part of D.J. James' cinema circuit along with the Mayfair and Upminster's Capitol, could hold 1,800 in red plush seats. There was a cafe and ballroom seating 200, with parking for a thousand cars. The grand opening by Cllr F.H.R. Davis, chairman of Hornchurch UDC, came on Saturday 3 August 1935. A stage show featuring Paul Lukas, 'the famous Hollywood Maestro de Dance', was followed by two films: Gordon Harker and Binnie Hale in *The Phantom Light* and Robert Young in *Vagabond Lady*. The proceeds from the opening performance went to worthy causes, with half being shared between the local division of the St John

The Towers Cinema not long after it opened in August 1935.

Ambulance Brigade and the Victoria Hospital, with the other half donated to the Hornchurch Social Services Association, to be used to provide food and clothing for the unemployed during the coming winter.

The Towers – telephone Hornchurch 700 – had a staff of around thirty under its first manager Mr G.E. Sewell, formerly manager of Upminster's Capitol. Several changes of ownership were experienced in the next decade. By 1939 the D.J. James' circuit – comprising the Mayfair, Capitol and Towers, along with Romford's Havana and Plaza, formerly owned by Victory Cinemas – had become part of Eastern Cinemas (GCF) Ltd and in 1943 these were taken over by the more extensive Odeon Theatres Limited. The Towers became part of the Rank Organisation in 1948, and two years later in 1950 was renamed the Odeon. It remained as the Odeon for almost twenty-five years until its closure as a cinema in October 1973, reopening as the Top Rank Bingo Club, later restyled as the Mecca Bingo, which it remains today.

During the Second World War the old cinema in Station Lane was at first used as a depot for medical supplies but later was called into service to store furniture from the numerous bombed-out buildings. By 1948 the lack of regular maintenance seems to have taken its toll and the premises were in very poor condition when they were bought by Hornchurch UDC. After considering several possible uses the council finally decided to set up a theatre there, refurbishing the former cinema and becoming the first local authority in Britain to take the lead in founding a professional theatre company. The Queen's Theatre, named in honour of the recently crowned monarch, was opened by Sir Ralph Richardson on 21 September 1953. Many actors who went on to become

The innovative Queen's Theatre in the 1950s.

household names were employed on the theatre repertory company over the following decades, including Anthony Hopkins, Glenda Jackson, Prunella Scales, Richard Briers and Wendy Craig. It continued as a community theatre until its closure in 1975, when the new Queen's Theatre in Billet Lane was opened and the old building demolished to make way for offices and shops.

The Billet Lane site had originally been earmarked for a civic centre for Hornchurch UDC. The new theatre was opened by Sir Peter Hall, then director of the National Theatre. The theatre's governing body is the charitable Havering Theatre Trust Limited (formerly the Hornchurch Theatre Trust). The London Borough of Havering remains the principal funding source, with additional grant aid from the education programme by the London Grants Committee and sponsorship from Save and Prosper Ltd. But the takings at the box-office are a key element in the theatre's viability. A permanent company of twelve actor-musicians has been recently re-established to perform the nine mainhouse and two Theatre-in-Education productions held annually. As well as running a community programme the theatre is a venue for local performing groups and a variety of concerts.

The Hornchurch UDC inherited from its predecessors a number of public parks. The first of these was the Park Lane Recreation Ground. In May 1924 the Romford RDC took a five-year lease on a 5½-acre piece of land in the heavily populated north-west Hornchurch, with the option to buy this for £1,375. This ground, used as a public playing field and also serving the local schools, was bought by Romford RDC and passed to Hornchurch UDC in 1926.

In 1925 local residents drew the rural council's attention to a large oval earth trotting track which was being laid out by a developer on a 22-acre site to the south of Osborne Road. The site had been bought in 1920 by the French family of the Oak Public House, Victoria Road, who originally used it for grazing and a piggery. The council tried to halt the plans of the developer, Mr Hastings of the Ebor Arms, Stoke Newington, to build a track, stands, stables and other facilities. The developer appealed to the Minister of Health to be allowed to continue. This led to a public inquiry in October 1925 when it was agreed that the council would open negotiations with the owners for acquiring it as an open space. But the Romford authorities had no intention of buying a site which would automatically transfer to the new Hornchurch Council in a few months.

In the meantime, the promoters carried on developing the trotting track, which would be used on occasions for athletics meetings too. The track opened with a race meeting supported by a large crowd on Whit Monday 1925. As well as temporary stalls for housing the horses on race days, there was a winning post and finishing enclosure, where the bookmakers and tic-tac men stood, backing onto the houses in Osborne Road. The whole area was enclosed by a corrugated iron fence. The meetings were supported by owners of trotting horses all over the country, and many horses would arrive a few days before the race meetings, coming by rail in special horse-boxes that

Hylands Park, Globe Road, former venue of a trotting track.

were shunted into the sidings in Victoria Road. There were six horses in each race, with the riders of the buggies wearing their respective owners' colours. Each race began with a rolling start, with competitors completing one lap of the quarter-mile track before the starter dropped his flag to get the four-lap races under way. Despite promising attendances early on, trotting meetings became gradually less well attended and the track was finally closed. The final purchase was completed by Hornchurch UDC in early 1927, and they developed it as a public park known as Hylands Park.

14. EDUCATION

In earlier times education was a privilege more usually reserved for the better off or as a result of a kindly benefactor's bequest. In Hornchurch the earliest education was provided by the local clergyman or in charity schools. In 1548 poor children were taught by priests appointed by Trinity Guild, while in the early 1620s boys were taught grammar by a curate. In the eighteenth century the opening of the Romford charity school in 1711 provided a few Hornchurch children with the opportunity to receive some education, while the founding of Aylett's school in 1731 under the will of Alice Aylett funded a schoolmaster to give tuition to ten poor boys.

In 1844 the National School was built next to the Chaplaincy on Church Hill, becoming the first elementary school in the village and accommodating boys, girls and

The former National School, North Street, is seen here on the right. *c.* 1908.

infants. This small building was later used by the Church Lads' Brigade as a drill hall. In March 1854 New College, Oxford, conveyed to the minister and churchwardens of Hornchurch land in North Street to be 'used as a school for education of children and adults or children only of the labouring manufacturing and other poorer classes in parish of Hornchurch'. The school was managed by a committee comprising the minister and four other practising members of the Church of England. In 1856 Aylett's school amalgamated with the National School. After the 1870 Education Act Hornchurch's National School was covered by the Board of Education's new funding arrangements, as well as annual inspections of the quality of instruction, learning and facilities by one of His Majesty's Inspectors.

In 1874 the boys left the original Church Hill school premises to move to a new school situated next to the teacher's house in North Street and able to accommodate up to 117 pupils. The old building was leased from the vicar and churchwardens for use by the infants during the day and for night classes on three evenings each week. The vicar also used the Church Hill premises as a Sunday school and, before its offices were built in Billet Lane in 1915, the parish council met there too. In 1886 a School Board was formed for Hornchurch.

Population growth in Victorian Hornchurch made the school accommodation in North Street inadequate for the needs of the village. In 1902 the Hornchurch School Board's plans for a new school for 200 boys and 200 girls, at a cost of almost £9,500, were approved. The new school in Westland Avenue was completed at the end of

February 1904, allowing the old girls' department to be converted for use by the infants, who moved out of their temporary accommodation.

In 1912 the Board of Education's inspector found the girls' school 'very pleasant' and the pupils 'very well behaved, neat and tidy in their work, appearance and interested in their lessons'. The boys' school inspection in 1920 reported that the 'boys read carefully and show intelligent grasp of the sense of fairly difficult English'.

From July 1921 North Street School took in older children from the Hornchurch Cottage Homes who had previously been taught at the Homes' separate school. This change was not a success as in 1924 the inspector felt that most of the sixty Cottage Homes girls, nearly one-third of the girls' school roll, were 'backward for their age' and that their presence seriously affected the organisation of the school and the quality of work. The school formed a 'special' class of older girls, made up mainly of those from the Cottage Homes.

The Hornchurch Cottage Homes had been built for children in their care by the Guardians of Shoreditch St Leonard's Poor Law Union on the 86-acre estate and farm of Harrow Lodge, bought from Edward Dawson in May 1886 for £6,300. The Guardians developed about 4 acres as a small-scale self-contained village of cottages, a school and other facilities at a cost of over £48,000. Some 60 acres were let to a local farmer and the rest kept to grow all the garden produce needed to support the homes.

At the opening ceremony on 28 August 1889, Professor Stuart MP described the buildings as places where 'the homeless would be brought up without the fear and away

One of the cottages at the Cottage Homes, Hornchurch.

from the shadow of the workhouse', allowing the children the chance to 'escape the taint of pauperism and to become faithful citizens of the country they loved', and to 'take the first step which would lead to a decent citizenship'.

At the entrance was a porter's lodge and a probationary ward in which newly arrived children spent two weeks before transferring to one of the cottage homes flanking the main avenue through the site. Each of the cottage homes – initially there were eleven with two added later – was meant to be a home in itself, housing up to thirty children in three rooms under the care of a foster mother. There was a school, a chapel, an infirmary, and an isolation hospital, where children were kept when suffering from one of the numerous infectious diseases common at that time. Each child attended elementary school before being trained in a 'suitable' trade. The girls learned 'household duties' under the instruction of their foster mother, while the boys were trained by an industrial tutor – usually the husband of one of the foster mothers – in either shoemaking and mending, painting and decorating, baking, gardening, or as a mechanic. The superintendent was in overall charge, James Cowley being the first at an initial salary of £170 p.a., with his wife, Elizabeth, employed as matron at £80 p.a.

Cottages were occupied either by girls and younger boys, or by boys alone. The girls' homes were named after flowers or plants (Hawthorne, Laurel, Woodbine, Rose, Ivy and Myrtle) and were usually looked after by a foster mother alone, helped by the older girls. The boys' homes had more masculine names of famous characters (Wellington, Nelson, Milton, Landseer and Napier) and were headed by both a foster mother and her husband. Life in the homes was the subject of the 1900 novel *A Son of the State* by Pett Ridge.

A group of young girls assemble outside the school, Hornchurch Cottage Homes, *c.* 1908.

Children leaving the homes were provided with clothing for their first year and regular checks were made on their progress. After leaving many boys entered Army or Navy service, some transferring to one of the training ships moored on the Thames, such as HMS *Goliath* or HMS *Chichester*. Many boys found places in military bands because of the training they had received in the homes' thriving band. At any time up to forty boys were in training under the eye of Matthew Larter, bandmaster until 1910, or his successor Henry Allden. However, the practice involved was not always viewed positively by the school inspector who in 1922 urged that 'if possible' the boys should 'not be taken for band practice during school hours'. The 'training' under the foster mother was meant to prepare the girls for domestic service, which most entered. But in 1909 the visiting school inspector reported that 'knowledge of domestic subjects is acquired in a somewhat casual and haphazard manner'.

Administratively, the Hornchurch Cottage Homes passed to the London County Council in 1930, transferring to the London Borough of Tower Hamlets when local government in London was reorganised in 1965. Changing practices in the 1970s led to more children being fostered in the community and a decreasing need for children's homes. Finally in 1984 the London Borough of Tower Hamlets closed the home and sold the site for development. Planning permission was granted for the development of 250 homes on the site, provided the Cottage Homes were restored and formed part of the scheme. A new housing development known as St Leonard's Hamlet sprang up during the late 1980s, but during the declining housing market of the early 1990s the developers dragged their heels on their commitment to restore the Victorian buildings, which gradually fell into disrepair. Following pressure from the local council and an upturn in the housing market, the former Cottage Homes, including the chapel, were converted into residential accommodation from 1993 onwards, securing the future of this unique part of Hornchurch's heritage.

As well as coping with children from the Cottage Homes in the 1920s, the North Street schools also had to contend with the rapid growth of Hornchurch's population and these continued to put pressure on the available accommodation. An extension of three additional classrooms for 150 scholars costing just under £3,000 was completed by the end of 1925, allowing the infants to transfer to the new buildings in January 1926 and finally vacate the old 1855 premises. But once again suburban growth led to serious overcrowding and, by the end of 1929, average attendance had increased by over 100 in just one year. In January 1930 plans for additional accommodation for 350 children were finalised, at an expected cost of £22,000, and 2½ acres were bought from New College, Oxford. But urgent steps were needed over the next year: the handicrafts and domestic classrooms were converted as temporary classrooms and children had to travel to the old British School at Upminster for these subjects; the church hall was hired to provide space for fifty-six scholars; four classrooms at the Hornchurch Cottage Homes were hired; in January 1931 the Baptist Hall was rented as a classroom for up to fifty girls.

The additional buildings were completed in April 1932 but by January 1933 there were 1,140 older boys and girls and 434 infants and these numbers could once again only be housed by renting the church hall and the Cottage Homes' classrooms. The opening of Suttons Lane School in April 1934 took the older children away and allowed the Westland Avenue School to be reorganised into junior and infants' schools, and the temporary premises were given up.

Scholars living around the South End Road in the south of the parish faced a lengthy walk to reach the village centre schools. This was remedied in 1864 when a school was built close to the current junction of South End Road and Wood Lane. The school was funded with income from Skeale's charity (set up under the will of Sibell Skeale in 1679), savings from National School funds, and subscriptions. It became known as Mrs Skeale's charity school and by 1871 sixty-three children were being taught there. In May 1889 the Hornchurch School Board continued the charity school as a public elementary school, renamed South Hornchurch Board School. With continued population growth additional space was needed and a new school with 150 places – 50 infants and 100 older children – was built a short distance away in Blacksmith's Lane at a cost of £3,300, opening on 29 May 1899. By late 1909 the school was already full and two extra classrooms providing seventy-four places were completed by January 1912.

The South Hornchurch schools appear to have had some educational problems. In May 1912 the inspector found 'a school of some difficulty. . . . The children seem slow in thinking and unresponsive.' By 1920 there were only three teachers for 179 children and the headmaster taught 72 children in five different standards. The inspector felt in 1926

Skeale's chapel and charity school, in South End Road, at the junction with Wood Lane. (London Borough of Havering)

that '. . . the majority of the children are probably below the average in mental ability' and that '. . . the general behaviour of the older children is rough and their manners are uncouth'. In 1929 the inspector concluded that 'there is not much evidence to show that the headmaster has any measurable influence in the working of the school'.

By autumn 1928 numbers in the schools had risen from 198 to 276 since March 1924. By March 1930 two extra classrooms costing £1,500 had been added for 100 extra children. At Easter 1934 about 130 older children were transferred to the newly opened Rainham Senior School, which allowed the Blacksmith's Lane School to be reorganised into infant and junior departments. Accommodation was still inadequate for the rising roll, with the school only a little to the south of the new Elm Park housing estate and with considerable residential development already taking place around the school. Extra land next to the school was bought in 1935 and the school was enlarged to cater for 450 children in 1937 and for 750 children in 1943. There were further enlargements in 1947 and again in 1964. When the new infants' school was built in Ford Lane the Blacksmith's Lane School became the junior school. These schools are now known as Whybridge Infants and Junior Schools.

By the 1890s the development of north-west Hornchurch parish was in full swing. The new Hornchurch School Board made a school for the area an early priority and in August 1891 brought forward plans for a school for 120 boys and 120 girls, as well as an infant department. The new Park Lane Board School opened on 4 September 1893, costing around £4,000. By 1904 the new Local Education Authority Essex County Council recognised the need to expand the school with about 160 extra places, the work being completed in June 1907.

The inspectors' reports were generally mixed but were rarely praiseworthy. The Park Lane School faced disruptions due to changes of teachers, unfilled vacancies, sickness epidemics among pupils and poor attendance. The teachers were criticised for doing too little to stretch the pupils or to prepare them for the future. In 1919 about twenty girls at the school were above the normal school leaving age and their standard of work was low, with little sign of progress. By 1923 a separate class of thirty-four 'dull and backward girls' following a simple and practical syllabus had been set up. Also in 1923 the boys were said to be 'somewhat rough in their ways and speech but . . . they are very keen on their sports'. In the infant school, the headteacher's liberal teaching methods 'brought out personality and (have) given self-confidence to the slow and backward' but reading and writing suffered and the experiment had been abandoned by 1926. The presence of Cottage Homes' children in the girls' and infants' school also had an adverse effect here, and it seems the school was affected by the attitude of some members of staff.

Pupil numbers rose by almost a quarter between December 1927 and September 1929, from 538 to 655. In June 1929 Hydesville Hall in Brentwood Road was hired for use by fifty senior girls until a 200-place portable building was provided in April 1930. The opening in 1930 of the new Hylands Senior School in Malvern Road for 400 pupils allowed the Park Lane School to be reorganised and in May 1935 the school was adapted

Children at Hornchurch Council School, Empire Day, early 1900s.

to provide for 446 junior, mixed and infant pupils. Until recently the premises had been used as a teachers' centre for Havering but it now houses Raphael Independent School.

During the 1920s the increased demand was met by adding places at existing schools but eventually new schools close to these new populations were needed. The housing development around Hornchurch Station from the late 1920s was followed by the opening of Sutton's Lane Junior School for 450 pupils in 1933. Rainsford Way School – now Wykeham – was opened in 1932 to serve the Haveringwell Estate to the west of Hornchurch. Developments to the north of Hornchurch necessitated the new Ardleigh Green School, which opened in 1934, while it was a few years after the development of the Elm Park Estate before the first school – Elm Park (later Benhurst Avenue) School – opened in 1936, with Ayloff School being built two years later. The first denominational school in the area was St Mary's Roman Catholic school, which opened on Hornchurch Road in 1933.

Senior schools followed within a few years. The Hylands School was enlarged and reorganised in 1935 for 560 senior boys while nearby the 450-place Bush Elms Senior School opened in Hyland Way in 1933. Dury Falls Mixed Senior School opened in 1935 with 500 places while the large 1,100-place Sutton's Lane Senior School opened in 1937, initially with two boys' and girls' departments. This later became Suttons Secondary Modern which was enlarged and renamed Sanders Draper School in 1973. The opening of Redden Court School in Harold Wood in 1939 led to the closure of the senior department of Ardleigh Green School.

15. RELIGION

Perfect described St Andrew's parish church as 'a grand and venerable pile . . . on top of the hill: hoary with age and weather-beaten with the storms, elemental and temporal'. Nothing much now remains from earlier than the thirteenth century but it is likely that as far back as the eleventh century, during the reign of Edward the Confessor (1042–66), the church at Hornchurch was the only one in the whole Liberty of Havering, except for the small chapel used exclusively by the royal household at the King's Palace at Havering-atte-Bower. Similarly, for many years Hornchurch churchyard was the only burial ground for the whole district. The parishioners of Romford had to bury their dead there until 1410 and those of Havering-atte-Bower until 1718.

Havering-atte-Bower already had long association with Saxon kings before Edward the Confessor made the royal bower or palace his own, often holding court there, and it is said that he died there on 5 January 1066. Although no firm evidence connects him with Hornchurch village or church, a legendary narrative links him to the supposed naming of Havering. The story relates that Edward was present at the consecration of a church in Essex when an old man begged alms of the king. Having no money, the king took off his ring and gave it to the beggar with the words 'Have a ring', which supposedly led to the name of Havering. This in turn has led some to suppose that the church concerned was at Hornchurch, and that the church was built by Edward himself. The legend is recalled in the stained-glass window in the eastern end of the north chancel. Other sources cite the church at Clavering.

Whatever the truth about the origins of St Andrew's church, it certainly existed in 1163 when Henry II gave it to the newly-founded priory of Hornchurch. The king presented 'the Hospice of St Bernard de Monte Jovis' of Savoy with property for the endowment of a religious house in Hornchurch in return for hospitality rendered by the order to the king's envoys while crossing the Alps. As a result a cell or hospice of St Nicholas and St Bernard, initially comprising a prior and twelve monks, was set up at Hornchurch, endowed by Henry II with the manors of Hornchurch Hall and Suttons. For the next 230 years priors and monks from the order lived at Hornchurch Priory until its dissolution in 1391. The exact location of the priory is unknown. One opinion was that it stood on the site of the old White Hart Inn, as the old inn contained some architectural remains of an ecclesiastical nature. Another view was that it may have been in the Mill Field by the churchyard, while a third placed it in Hornchurch village at the junction of North Street and the High Street.

In 1253 the priory was described as 'the horned Monastery' (in Latin: *Monasterio Cornuto*). Morant, the eighteenth-century Essex historian, conjectured that the bull's head and horns may have been the crest of the religious house of Savoy but this is unlikely. Certainly by 1384 a bull's head and horns appear on the seal of the prior of Hornchurch and the village had been known as 'Hornechirche' for over a century.

The origins of the parish church of St Andrew, Hornchurch, date from at least 1163.

In 1391 William of Wykeham, Bishop of Winchester, bought the priory and its possessions as part of his endowment of New College, Oxford, which had been completed in 1387. In return the college ordained a minister for Hornchurch. Although this incumbent was neither a rector nor a vicar but was correctly styled a chaplain and vicar temporal, he is usually described as a vicar. In keeping with this, his residence was neither a rectory nor a vicarage but a private house owned by New College, known as 'The Chaplaincy'. The right to appoint a vicar rests with New College and the incumbent was traditionally a former New College scholar.

The college also had peculiar jurisdiction in the parish, which meant that the bishop of the diocese had no authority there. At the periodic visitations by the archdeacon, for instance, the Hornchurch vicar formally refused entry, although allowing admission to the church informally, as a matter of courtesy. This remained the situation well into the nineteenth century. Only after Revd Herbert Dale's incumbency from 1902 was the situation altered and the Bishop of St Alban's, Dr Edgar Jacob (himself a New College man), became the first bishop of the diocese for over 500 years to enter the church in his own right, instead of at the invitation of the incumbent.

Hornchurch parish was originally one and the same as Havering Liberty, and Hornchurch's church was known as the church of Havering. The current church owes its origins to the thirteenth century when it was completely rebuilt, possibly as early as 1220. Arcades in the nave and the triple sedilia in the chancel are the only remains of that period. Work was put in hand soon after New College obtained the benefice. Early in the fifteenth century the chancel and the aisles were rebuilt, and later in the same century the chapels, clerestory and north porch were added. The tower had been planned by 1476 and was completed by 1491–2. The roofs of the chancel, north chapel, nave and north aisle appear to date from the same period. The spire was probably added in the following century.

In 1716 pews were added and other work gave the church interior the appearance of one of Wren's City churches, with a richly carved wooden pulpit, a reredos in the style

Interior of St Andrew's church, *c.* 1916.

of Grinling Gibbons, a panelled chancel, and a west gallery. A significant change occurred in 1802 when the lead covering of the spire was replaced by copper. During this partial restoration, the south aisle and chancel were rebuilt at the same time. The tower and spire, which rise to a height of 120 feet, had for many years been one of the landmarks used by shipping on the Thames, and this change, which led to the spire acquiring its distinctive green tinge, no doubt enhanced its usefulness.

Major restorations were carried out between 1869 and 1871. In 1869 New College restored the chancel, inserting a new east window in memory of Thomas Mashiter JP. Two years later in 1871, during the incumbency of Revd Thomas Griffiths, the church was restored at a cost of £2,000. The changes included: a new chancel arch; a new arch to the south chapel; a new stone pulpit, font and reredos; and new heating apparatus. The piscina, sedilia, and vestry screen were restored, stonework restored throughout and windows reglazed. At the same time the grand fittings from the Georgian era, including the fine old carved oak pulpit and the high-backed pews, were removed. While these restorations were underway from May 1871 church services were held in the nearby tithe barn at Hornchurch Hall. Further renovations costing £950 were carried out in 1896, including re-leading the south aisle roof. Subsequent changes were the addition of a choir vestry in 1913 and the rebuilding of the eastern gable of the chancel in 1921.

It is on this east gable that Hornchurch's famous motif, the stone Highland bull's head and hollow copper horns, was to be seen until it was stolen in July 1999. Although firm references date from no earlier than 1824, as early as 1610 there is a record of 'points of lead fashioned like horns'. Given that the church was known as the 'horned church'

The bull's head on the ivy-covered east gable of St Andrew's.

before the thirteenth century it is possible that this device is of much older origins, perhaps associated in some way with Hornchurch's leather industry.

St Andrew's was originally the church that served the whole Liberty of Havering, covering Romford and Havering as well as Hornchurch. Havering-atte-Bower only gained its full independence from Hornchurch as a separate parish in the 1780s while Romford had to wait until 1849 to achieve a similar status. But this still left St Andrew's church to serve a large, diverse and rapidly growing parish.

A chapel of ease to St Andrew's church was built at South Hornchurch in 1864 to serve the growing community in the distant south of the parish. It was enlarged by the addition of a chancel in 1882, the gift of Revd Robert Johnson, vicar of Hornchurch, and Mrs Helme. This chapel, built of yellow stock bricks with a slate roof, stood on the east side of South End Road, directly opposite Wood Lane, and also housed Sibell Skeale's charity school. Services were conducted by a lay preacher and in 1923 the preacher, Mr J.T. Attwooll, had acted in that capacity for twenty-seven years. The chapel later became the mission church of St John, under St Andrew's Hornchurch, and continued in use even after it was bought by Hornchurch UDC for potential demolition as part of their road-widening scheme in 1939. It was closed to public use in May 1941 when the RAF closed off South End Road, enclosing the chapel within the airfield boundaries. Shortly afterwards the priest-in-charge visited the premises with the RAF chaplain and retrieved the altar, a stone font and four pews, all of which were transferred to St Nicholas, Elm Park. The chapel was finally demolished late in 1955. A new church, dedicated to St

John and St Matthew, was built in 1957 on a site further to the south on South End Road. This site, which was bought by the church authorities, had been previously occupied by the Strong Memorial Hall, destroyed by enemy action in April 1941.

The large population in north-west Hornchurch had no church of their own prior to the First World War, their spiritual needs being ministered to by St Andrew's Romford. When Revd Charles Steer became vicar of Hornchurch in 1918 he soon concluded that the area needed its own church. In August 1919 it was decided to buy a plot of land at the corner of Malvern Road and Park Lane for £200 as a site for a temporary building. A hut formerly used by the New Zealand contingent as a chapel at Grey Towers camp was bought and removed, re-erected and equipped at the new site early in 1920, at a cost of £365. This served not only as a mission church but also as the Church Army Social Centre until 1922, when the church bought out their interest. The hut became used only for church services and social work, with the Revd T. Cragge appointed as the first curate-in-charge, although he soon resigned because of ill health. At the same time a 2-acre site in a prominent position on the corner of Park Lane and Hornchurch Road was secured for a future permanent church.

The name Holy Cross was first applied to the hut in April 1923 and Holy Cross became a parish in its own right, formed out of St Andrew's, in 1925. Revd John B. Carlos, previously priest-in-charge of St Mary Magdalene, East Ham, took up the appointment as the first vicar of Holy Cross in February 1926. The first building on the new site was a temporary church hall, initially used as a Sunday school. On 10 December

The temporary church of Holy Cross, Malvern Road, formerly the chapel at Grey Towers Camp.

1932 the Bishop of Chelmsford conducted a ceremony to lay the foundation stone. The last service in the old hut was held on 14 September, after which it was known as Malvern Hall. The new church was consecrated two days later before a congregation of 600, many having to stand as the church was designed to hold only 450. The first vicarage (now No. 258 Hornchurch Road), built in 1930–1, was sold in 1949 and between 1950 and 1958 the vicar, Revd Peter Thompson, and his family lived at No. 163 Park Lane. Revd Thompson was vicar for almost thirty years, retiring in 1978. During that time he devoted considerable energy to the nearby Cottage Homes, of which he was chaplain, and to its former residents. Being a non-driver, he walked everywhere and became a familiar figure, making his way home from visits, often late at night.

The other Anglican parish is that of St Nicholas, Elm Park. This had its origins in a temporary building erected in 1936, which was used for many years for church services and youth and community meetings. In 1956 a permanent church was built, and the following year St Nicholas became a parish in its own right, created out of St Andrew's. Two mission churches are attached to St Andrew, Hornchurch: St George, Kenilworth Gardens, originally built as a mission hall in 1931 and extended into a church by the addition of a chancel in 1935; and St Matthew, Chelmsford Drive, built in 1956.

Of the nonconformists the Baptists have the strongest links in Hornchurch. In November 1877 a small band of Baptists, who had met in a mission hall off the High Street, decided to explore the possibility of forming a Baptist church for Hornchurch.

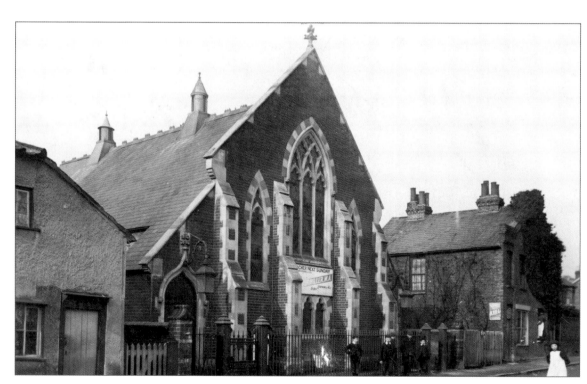

The former Baptist church, North Street, seen here c. 1906, was opened in 1882.

A Church Fellowship was formed, with fourteen signatories, in February 1878 and over the next four years the congregation grew so much that larger premises were needed. John Abraham of Upminster Windmill presented a site in North Street, on which a 220-place church was built. The memorial stone was laid by Mr Abraham on 18 July 1882, and the famous Baptist preacher Revd Charles Spurgeon was the principal speaker at the ceremony. The new church was opened for worship on 21 September 1882, and was enlarged to provide seating for 270 in 1903. Further enlargements and modernisations were carried out between 1931 and 1936. The Baptist church in North Street welcomed other nonconformist worshippers.

The Ardleigh Green Baptist church, in Ardleigh Green Road, originated in 1914 as a mission to the main Hornchurch Baptist church. It originated in a temporary hut, donated by Mr R. Banyard. A permanent brick church, able to accommodate 260 worshippers, was built and furnished in 1933 at a cost of around £1,500. Mr Banyard also gave part of the site, the rest being donated by Messrs Thomas England and E.G. Pearson. The Elm Park Baptist church in Rosewood Avenue was formed in 1937, supported by the Hornchurch Baptist church and the Essex Baptist Association, with house meetings and a Sunday school. A school-chapel was built in 1938 but suffered bomb damage in 1940. The current church was built in 1963.

Hornchurch's Congregational church, Nelmes Road, was formed in 1906. The first services were held on 13 May that year in a small schoolroom at 'Cosy Cot', Ernest Road, holding up to forty people. The following month the church was affiliated to the London Congregational Union, and was supported by the Romford Congregational church. In October 1906 the church acquired a much larger room, to hold up to ninety people, at Gladstone House, at the junction of Berther Road and Butts Green Road, continuing there until September 1909. Early in 1909 a site had been acquired in Nelmes Road and a church with accommodation for 230 was built, the costs met through the generosity of the late Thomas Dowsett of Southend-on-Sea. This formally opened on 23 September 1909. The church is now known as Nelmes United Reformed church.

Although Hornchurch had a sizeable Methodist congregation meeting in a house – possibly the Hollies in North Street – during the 1830s, it was only in 1929 that the Hornchurch (Wesleyan) Methodist church in the High Street originated with meetings in the Masonic Hall. A school-chapel was built in 1933 and the current church was built in 1958. The Grenfell Hall Methodist church on the Haveringwell Estate can be traced to house meetings in the early 1930s. A two-storey church was developed in 1936 on a site given by Thomas England, the estate developer. The Elm Park Methodist church was opened in Mungo Park Road in 1957.

The first Roman Catholic church in Hornchurch parish was the church of St Mary, which was opened in Hornchurch Road in 1931 and consecrated two years later. Subsequently the provision for Roman Catholic worship was expanded in 1955 when the church of the English Martyrs, Alma Avenue, was founded. The church of St Alban, Langdale Gardens, opened in 1960.

16. Elm Park – 'The Wonder-town of Homes'

According to developers Richard Costain Ltd, Elm Park was to be 'the Wonder-town of homes – incomparably complete and ideally situated – built upon the one-time wheat-fields of open Essex'. Costain's master plan for the 560-acre development in South Hornchurch envisaged a country town of 7,000 homes, five shopping centres, eight schools, two churches, 'a model inn', a 3,000-seater cinema, and its own station offering direct travel to London. It was to be the single largest private housing enterprise yet attempted in Britain, housing between 25,000 and 30,000 people.

By the early 1930s Costain were already estate developers of some renown, with major sites around London including the 1,460-home Brentwater centre, south of the Welsh Harp, the 'model estate' of 1,250 at Croham Heights near Croydon, the Sudbury Hill Estate comprising 1,150 homes, and the Kingswood 'Country Estate' in Surrey. But the 7,000-home Elm Park proposals dwarfed anything attempted by the company before and was far larger than any other private development locally.

Costain's Elm Park Estate was mainly developed on two farms, Wyebridge Farm and Elm Farm. Of sixteenth-century origins, Wyebridge Farm stood on the east side of Upper Rainham Road, just north of the railway line, and comprised some 270 acres. Together with Maylards Farm, whose name had by the eighteenth century become corrupted into Maylands, Wyebridge had formed part of the manor of Maylards Green and Wyebridge. Until 1913 both farms had been owned by the family of the Marquis of Salisbury but they were then sold and passed into separate hands. Wyebridge was bought for £7,600 by Edward Winmill, and it was his family who sold the farm to Costain Ltd for £53,100 in June 1933, with Cheke and Co. of Romford the selling agents.

The second large holding bought by Costain was the 199-acre holding directly east of Wyebridge Farm, mainly comprising the 96-acre Elm Farm, which straddled the South End Road, and the 65-acre Uphavering Farm, which was split in two by the London, Tilbury and Southend Railway line (Abbs Cross Secondary School lies on the part north of the railway). In the late nineteenth century the farms had been owned by the Rickards family before they were sold to Walter Vellacott of West Thurrock in 1913. Robert Beard bought the farms for £35,000 in October 1931 and within two years made a £20,000 profit, finally selling on to Costains in July 1933, through John Read, estate agent.

The proposals for the new Elm Park Estate were announced in May 1933 and plans for the site's development were brought forward the following month. As part of the planning agreement with Hornchurch Urban District Council, Costain Ltd agreed to

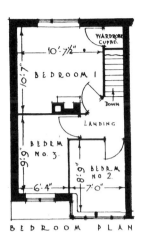

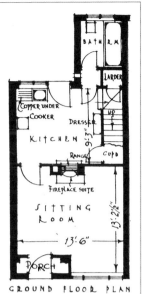

"The **HAWTHORNE**"
HOME   **(End Type)**

**Building
Society
Repayments** **12/3** WEEKLY
BUYS

RATES ADD APPROXIMATELY 3/6 WEEKLY

BEDROOM PLAN

Again in the end house six full-sized rooms, and the attributes of a semi-detached are afforded. These positions will be readily sought after and should be reserved by those requiring accommodation for garages, where this is possible, without delay.

Sanitary fittings are glistening white porcelain enamel of the best quality with Chromium plated fittings. Copper pipes are fitted as in all other types ensuring neat fixing and greater protection from frost.

The porch is a feature of this type affording greater protection to the entrance door, and place for pram to stand during inclement weather.

GROUND FLOOR PLAN

£437
FREEHOLD

Cash deposit **£15 0 0**
12 weeks at 17s. 4d. **£10 8 0**
during occupation
Building Society
Advance **£411 12 0**
Repayments **£2 9s.** per lunar
month or **12s. 3d.** weekly.
Full deposit of **£25 8s.** can be
paid if desired to benefit.
Special rates of repayments on a
smaller scale can be given where
desirable to increase cash deposit.

Advertisement from Costain's brochure for the Hawthorne Home, mid-1930s. (David Parish)

transfer 81 acres of the former Wyebridge Farm as a gift to the council; this became part of Harrow Lodge Park. In addition it was agreed that they would build a 40-foot bridge over the railway, surrender land for widening the South End and Rainham Roads, and plant trees and shrubs on the estate. The district council's decision to vary the town planning scheme to allow a higher density than usual of thirteen-and-a-half houses per acre caused a long-running political row locally.

Work began in January 1934 when a temporary office was set up at Wyebridge Farm and the company started recruitment, promising to engage all staff via the local labour exchange. By June 1934 Costains were advertising that homes 'in choicest positions adjoining new station site now ready for inspection' from only 11s weekly. The official estate opening came on Saturday 18 May 1935, sixteen months after its commencement, when the Minister for Health Sir E. Hilton Young performed the ceremony, after first opening with a silver key the gates of the new railway station built on the District Line specially to meet the needs of the estate. Over 3,000 visitors travelled to Elm Park from the East End on a 'luxury train' at Costain's expense, to be met on arrival by a white concrete arch bearing the words 'Welcome to Hornchurch' and the Hornchurch coat of arms. Over 500 houses had already been built and 'queues lined up waiting to view the compact modern-looking houses'.

The earliest developments were north of the railway line, along the west-east route of Elm Park Avenue 'from the tree-bordered Rainham Road to the eastern boundary of Abbs Cross Road' which Costain claimed were 'selling on sight'. Warren Drive (originally named Park Avenue) marked the northern boundary and by spring 1936 good progress had been made in developing St Nicholas, Benhurst, Eyhurst, and Wodecote Avenues within this northern part of the estate. The majority of houses had five rooms – sitting-room, kitchen, and three bedrooms – with others conforming to the perhaps more usual pattern of two reception rooms, kitchen and three bedrooms. The most common – and cheapest – house was the five-roomed terraced 'Bramblewood', which sold for £395 freehold, with mortgage repayments of 11s weekly. Its modern fittings included a 'dresserette' with folding table, gas copper for washing, a gas cooker, Crittals 'steel casement windows in wood surrounds', with electricity laid on, complete with 'Bakelite switches and door fittings'. An end-terrace 'Bramblewood' cost £412 – just £17 (or 6d weekly) more, and 'the side entrance affords all the advantages of a semi-detached house . . . in some instances even to the extent of room for a garage for small motorcar or motorbike'. For just £420 or 11s 9d weekly, purchasers could acquire the terraced six-roomed 'Hawthorne' type house,

Chauffeurs wait at the bus-stop at Roneo Corner to ferry potential purchasers to the Elm Park Estate, mid-1930s. (David Parish)

Elm Park Broadway shopping parade, late 1930s.

A similar view to the photograph above, looking south towards Elm Park Station from Elm Park Avenue, 1960s.

while the slightly dearer end-terrace version sported an entrance porch with space for a 'pram to stand during inclement weather'. The top-of-the-range house was the seven-roomed 'Rosewood', also in terrace and end-terrace versions at £522 and £548 freehold respectively. Exteriors were less uniform than the other styles, and some were built with bay windows. Some semi-detached houses were offered, with the 'Premier Type' accommodation of the Elm Park Bungalow (14s 6d weekly), the 'Villette' (15s 6d), and the top-of-the-range 'Chalet' (at 18s 6d weekly) adding some variety and better quality housing.

To boost early sales a special Bank Holiday Home Exhibition was held in August 1935. Callers at Costain's estate office at No. 8 Station Parade, East Ham were enticed with free rail tickets to Elm Park and a free invitation to tea while there. But perhaps the best incentive was that costs were lower, with the terraced 'Bramblewood' house offered for just 10s 3d weekly, 9d cheaper than before, and the 'Hawthorne' terraced house down to 10s 9d, a 1s reduction on the original price. Purchasers' removal costs were also paid.

But once the estate began to be occupied the new residents' pleasure at their new home in the country were outweighed by the reality of living there. Among the genuine complaints in February 1938, almost three years after the development had opened, were a lack of post-boxes, with people on the south side having a twenty-minute walk to the nearest one, and just one telephone kiosk to serve 2,000 houses. There was no bus service on the estate: a bus service that had once run through the estate was discontinued without notice, leaving some residents with a quarter-hour walk to the bus route. At first there was no recreation ground and educational facilities were inadequate, with only one temporary school, accommodating 450 to 500 pupils, opening in 1936. By September 1937 the school roll had increased to 734 and the newly opened Assembly Hall had to be pressed into use as an emergency measure in September 1937 for 160 children. There were no facilities for a senior school, with the nearest at Suttons Lane, Hornchurch, reached either by train or by a half-hour walk. By the outbreak of war about three-quarters of the planned estate had been built.

The Elm Park shopping centre developed over several years. At first, shops were in pre-fabricated buildings but permanent premises were built on the west side of the road from the station down the hill. By December 1936 the new Broadway Parade included Beitler's bakery ('bread cut to any thickness free of charge'), the Elm Park Electrical, Sports and Radio Stores, Levine's Chemists, Hollick's newsagent, tobacconist and stationer (who offered a lending library at 2d per week) and Delin's grocery stores. The post office was a small counter in a shop known as the Tuck Box, opposite Elm Park Hotel. By January 1938 the shops were 'fast nearing completion' and four months later in May 1938 the local press reported that the shopping centre had been 'nearly completed', with builders hard at work to complete shops in time for Whitsun openings. One such Whitsun opening was the Woolworth store on Elm Park Avenue, which opened on 27 May. The first pub to be built was the Elm Park Hotel, which

Looking north, the Elm Park Hotel is on the left.

opened in July 1938 a little later than planned as work had been delayed while a bed of sand 20 feet deep was removed before foundations could be laid. This site had previously been used as a temporary play site for children. The promised 3,000-seater cinema, on a site bought by D.J. James' Circuit (owners of the Capitol in Upminster and Hornchurch's Towers), opposite the station, had not been built by the time war intervened and never materialised afterwards, once television took a hold. The planned library was only built in 1956.

The estate received unwelcome national publicity in January 1939 over the murder of nine-year-old Pamela Coventry, whose naked body was found in a ditch at the side of Wood Lane. She had left her home in Morecambe Close after lunch on 18 January to return to Benhurst Avenue School but failed to arrive. Two weeks later a 28-year-old father of two from nearby Coronation Drive was arrested and charged with her murder. At the trial at the Old Bailey at the end of March 1939 he was acquitted, as the evidence was circumstantial with no direct links to the accused.

After the war, work on the southern part of the estate restarted. It was only at this time that the shopping centre was finally extended to the east side of the road, and shops were built on the undeveloped parts of Elm Park Avenue, which had previously been used as allotments.

ACKNOWLEDGEMENTS

Except where otherwise stated all the illustrations in this book are from my photograph and postcard collection. I am very grateful to those who made other photographs available, whose names are indicated in the appropriate captions, and who gave me permission to use them. In addition particular thanks go to: Jane Finnett and other staff at Romford Central Reference Library who helped with my research; Jeanne Baker, for help with the history of Hornchurch's iron industry and her biographical article 'Charles Thomas Perfect, 1864–1939' in *Romford Record*, 31 (1998); Mr Derek Standen, regarding the Standen family; Mr Tony and Bill Carter, for assistance regarding their ancestor William Carter; Mr Bob Brannon, London Borough of Havering, for allowing me access to the borough's deeds collection; and Mrs Wyn Davis and Mr Frederick Aley, for information on old Hornchurch.

BIBLIOGRAPHICAL SOURCES

BOOKS

Ballard, Ted, *Our old Romford and district*, Upminster, Swan Libraries, 1981

Benton, Tony, *Upminster and Hornchurch in old photographs*, Stroud, Sutton Publishing, 1997

Booker, John, *Essex and the Industrial Revolution*, Chelmsford, Essex County Council, 1974

Bowyer, Chaz, *For Valour: The Air VCs*, London, William Kimber, 1992

Butler, Anthony, *The Hornchurch story*, Upminster, Swan Library, 1970

Carter, Herbert Spencer, *I call to mind*, Poole, Author, 1949

Dorlay, J.S., *The Roneo story*, Roneo Vickers, 1978

Elm Park local history infopack, Havering, Havering School Library Service, 1992

Evans, Brian, *Bygone Hornchurch and Upminster*, Chichester, Phillimore, 1990

——, *Hornchurch and Upminster, a pictorial history*, Chichester, Phillimore, 1996

Holy Cross Church, Hornchurch, Hornchurch, Holy Cross Church, 1983

Hough, Richard and Richard, Denis, *The Battle of Britain: the jubilee history*, Hodder and Stoughton, 1989

Humby, Gordon, *The Queen's Theatre, Hornchurch: a history*, 1998

Lewis, Frank, *History of Rainham, Wennington and South Hornchurch*, Romford, Ian Henry Publications, 1985

Mannox, Barbara, *Hornchurch and the New Zealand connection*, Havering, Havering Library Service, 1993

——, *The making of Emerson Park*, Havering, Havering Library Service, 1990

Peaty, Ian P., *Essex brewers*, 1992

Perfect, Charles Thomas, *History of the ancient parish church of St Andrew, Hornchurch*, Colchester, Benham, 1923

——, *Hornchurch during the Great War*, Colchester, Benham, 1920

——, *Our village*, Hornchurch, Perfect, 1912

——, *Ye olde village of Hornchurch*, Colchester, Benham, 1917

Smith, Eric, *First things first: RAF Hornchurch and RAF Suttons Farm 1915–1962*, Romford, Ian Henry Publications, 1992

Smith, Graham, *Essex airfields in the Second World War*, Newbury, Countryside Books, 1996

Stout, Victoria, *Around Kinson Pottery*, Poole, Author, 1992

Victoria County History of Essex, Volume VIII, 1983

Weightman, Gavin and Humphries, Steve, *The making of modern London 1914–1939*, Sidgwick and Jackson, 1984

ARTICLES

Numerous articles in *Havering History Review*, particularly the series by L.A. Aves in the 1970s, and in *Romford Record*

OTHER SOURCES

Thomas Wilson's scrapbooks on the history of Upminster and Hornchurch (Essex Record Office, T/P 67, volumes 1–14)

Cuttle Local Government Collection (Essex Record Office, T/P 181/6/27)

Romford Rural District Council Minutes, 1898 onwards (Romford Reference Library)

Census 1841–91 (Romford Reference Library)

Local newspapers 1894 onwards (Romford Reference Library)

Board of Education files (Public Record Office, class ED21)

Valuation Office Survey 1910–15 (Public Record Office, class IR58)

Hornchurch Cottage Homes records (London Metropolitan Archives, Sh.B.G.)

INDEX